F/04

400

THE LIFE AND WRITINGS OF
JOHN BUNYAN

THE STATUE OF JOHN BUNYAN AT BEDFORD
PRESENTED BY THE DUKE OF BEDFORD TO THE TOWN IN 1874
Sir J. Edgar Boehm, Sculptor

The

Life and Writings

of

JOHN BUNYAN

By HAROLD E. B. SPEIGHT

PROFESSOR OF PHILOSOPHY
PROFESSOR-ELECT OF BIOGRAPHY
DARTMOUTH COLLEGE

WITH AN INTRODUCTION BY

FRANCIS GREENWOOD PEABODY

Plummer Professor of Christian Morals,
Emeritus, Harvard University

NEW YORK and LONDON

HARPER & BROTHERS *Publishers*

ANNO M·CM·XXVIII

TO THE MEMORY OF

E.S.

A MODERN
MR. VALIANT-FOR-TRUTH

AND OF

G.G.

A MODERN MR. STAND-FAST

FOR BOTH OF THESE PILGRIMS
"ALL THE TRUMPETS SOUNDED ON THE OTHER SIDE."

CONTENTS

✠

vii

ILLUSTRATIONS

✠

INTRODUCTION

The Pilgrim's Progress from this World to that which Is to come is one of the most astonishing miracles of literary history. What could be more improbable than that a strolling tinker, with no literary training except in the Bible, with no knowledge of the world beyond walking distance of Bedford, and with twelve years spent in prison as a disturber of the peace, should have produced a masterpiece, of which Macaulay could affirm that it was the most popular religious writing in the English language? Indeed, this little book is a miracle even among Bunyan's own writings. Who has ever read, or cared to read, his *Life and Death of Mr. Badman,* or his *Sighs From Hell, or the Groans of a Damned Soul?* Even his *Grace Abounding,* though a vivid and genuine confession, has too much in it of "Bemoaning My Sad and Doleful State" to appeal to the modern mind. A crude and unmitigated Puritanism is not redeemed even by fertile fancy or nimble wit. Then, as out of a heap of rubbish, springs the beautiful flower of religious romance, which has remained fragrant and unfading for three hundred years.

What is the secret of this unparalleled efflores-. cence? Much is due no doubt to its plan—so dramatic, picturesque, intimate and personalized. Bunyan's method is that of the parables of Jesus. He does not tell what sins and vices are; he tells what they are like. Life, he says, is a pilgrimage; and human foibles and vices meet one on his way as persons whom one greets and can call by name. It is one thing to commend honesty, and quite another thing to write, "Well said, Father Honest, for by this I know thou art a cock of the right kind." It is one thing to say of courage that it overcomes difficulties, and quite another thing to say of Mr. Great-heart, "When he came to the Hill Difficulty he made no stick at that, nor did he much fear the lions." The abstract qualities thus disguised as plain English folk, still in modern attire beset the road to the City of the King. Mr. Worldly Wiseman, and Mr. Facing-bothways are still to be met on Sunday at church and on week days in business. Mr. Light-mind and Mr. Formality are as beguiling and persuasive as ever. Great-heart and Valiant-fortruth are still guides across the "Enchanted

Ground." All this is not only entertaining and vivacious as the report of a venturesome journey, but it converts preaching into story-telling and experience into romance.

When one turns from the form to the spirit of the parable, the first effect is, it must be confessed, not alluring. Bunyan's Pilgrim is a self-centred and ungenerous kind of Christian, primarily concerned not with building the City of God, but with escaping from the City of Destruction. Wife and neighbours are left to their fate without a pang. Christian is a runaway, not a saviour. Of the finer traits of sacrifice, compassion, and self-forgetfulness, Bunyan has little to teach. He has forgotten what was said of his Master, "He saved others, himself he cannot save." Christian wants to be rid of his burden, not to carry his own cross.

On the other hand, this tale of the soul's vicissitudes has a peculiar timeliness when, after three hundred years, the discipline of the inner life is so largely forgotten in the affairs of the working world, when introspection is displaced by action and meditation merged in service. The larger scope of modern morals and the testifying to consecration by compassion, significant as they are as signs of a healthier faith, depend after all on the integrity and constancy of the soul itself. "Only he can give who has," Emerson said. "The men on whom the soul descends alone can teach." It is a good time to remember the hindrances which beset, not the world alone, but the progress of the soul; a good time to face Mr. Obstinate and Mr. Timorous and to escape from Mr. Self-conceit and Mr. Discontent. Christian, it is true, is a most imperfect type of piety, but Christiana redeems the whole story with her devotion, and we stand with undiminished reverence among the throng which gathers to see her take her journey. "So she came forth and entered the river with a beckon of farewell to those that followed her to the river side. The last word she was heard to say here was, 'I come, Lord, to be with Thee and bless Thee!'"

In a word, the survival of *Pilgrim's Progress* is a convincing evidence of the unexhausted interest and permanent appeal of personal religion. The modern reader may find some of the hindrances that beset Christian artificial or extinct. He may not fall in with "the foul fiend," Apollyon, who "straddled quite over the whole breadth of the way" and threw "a flaming dart" at Pilgrim's heart. But no one can go far on life's journey without slipping into a Slough of Despond, or climbing a Hill Difficulty, or meeting the man "in the Iron Cage of Despair"; and it may even happen to one some day that the burden he is carrying may be "loosed from his shoulders and tumble until it is seen no more." A story of the soul's adventures is timeless in its appeal. Life for every serious mind is a pilgrimage "from the world that is to that which is to come"; and he who, even in homely pictures and antique theology, tells the true tale of that inner life has justly earned his literary immortality.

FRANCIS G. PEABODY.

PREFACE

THE unsuccessful attempt of the Stuart kings and their advisers to compel uniformity of worship and religious opinion in seventeenth-century England, which involved, of course, the silencing of the voice of private judgment and conscience, drove out of the Church of England many of her most devout and discerning souls. Dissenting groups, born of protest, flourished with the characteristic vigour of dissent, and to this day they have nourished the religious life of the more enterprising and more earnest elements in the working-class and middle-class population of England and Wales. The National Church has been national in quite a limited sense, through the possession of statutory privileges and through its associations with the monarchy, the aristocracy (its bishops being seated in the House of Lords), the military and naval establishments, and certain of the older institutions of learning. Perhaps it is not extreme to say that the sentiment favourable to disestablishment to-day is part of the price

which the English Church has paid for its in-
hospitality to Puritanism and to those later re-
vivals of personal religion, like the Methodist
movement, which were inspired by similar motives.

The Church paid a heavy price for whatever
advantage it gained through political intrigue
and for such material prosperity as it acquired
when it lost sight of the task for which it was
created. How great was this price it has not
learned until these later years. Puritanism was
the inevitable protest of an aroused conscience,
and Puritanism was, for the Church, a costly
reaction, for the Christian conscience of England found its expression thereafter through
those dissenting communions which owe their
existence to one or another of the blunders of
the Church. Not until comparatively recent
times did the Establishment again play any notable part in the moral leadership of the people
of England.

On the other hand, the cost of protest was a
very serious one for those men and women who
resisted the tyranny of the Act of Uniformity
of 1662, the Conventicle Act of 1664, the
Five Mile Act of 1665, and other provisions of
the "Clarendon Code" intended to stamp out

Preface

every variety of Independency. Many left the country to seek freedom in distant colonies; thousands of others filled the jails of England rather than submit. Their experiences were a fresh baptism of loyalty to one who had himself withstood, even to death, the formalists, political schemers, and exploiters of ecclesiastical power, and who had shown to men a "new and living way."

Such suffering for conscience' sake and such a reaffirmation of the meaning of Christianity for everyday life would not, however, have made so signal a contribution to religious development if there had not appeared a spokesman capable of voicing the convictions of these men and women in the spiritual vernacular of practical and personal religion. Such a man was raised up in John Bunyan, who called himself a "brasier" but was ridiculed as a "tinker." He was born late in the year 1628 in the hamlet of Harrowden beside the village of Elstow, near the town of Bedford. Before he died in 1688, the year that saw the coming of William III to end the Stuart misrule, a hundred thousand copies of the book by which he is best known had been circulated in cheap editions within the reach of poor people. "It is not until we reach Bunyan and George Fox, and catch at last the authentic voices of men of the people, unlettered and un-Latined, that we learn what the Reformation had meant." [1]

The story of John Bunyan is the story of a man despised by the gentry but heard gladly by the common people in an age which saw their almost complete neglect by the official representatives of Christianity; it is the story of a man who could match his wits with learned judges and leave them baffled, a man who preferred twelve years of prison to any surrender of principle, and when in prison assiduously laboured to support his family and minister to the souls of his fellow sufferers, a man who from his prison sent out writings which achieved a popularity he would have been the last to expect and a translation into tongues of which he never heard. When we look back over the course of three hundred years to estimate afresh our debt to men who gave us so many of the liberties we enjoy and who gave to Protestantism its central concern for religious experience we may well find it worth our while to tell and to

---

[1] T. R. Glover, *Poets and Puritans*, p. 115.

hear yet once more the story of the man who described himself on the title page of one of his books as "that Poor Contemptible Creature John Bunyan of Bedford."

The literature on the subject of Bunyan and his books, as is indicated in the Bibliography, is extensive. Acknowledgment has been made in the chapters that follow of the books that have been most helpful; many others have been consulted. The ultimate source of information is, of course, Bunyan's own work, and as far as possible he has been allowed to tell his own story. No claim of novelty is made for the interpretations of his allegories in their reference to personal religion; the consideration of *Pilgrim's Progress* in the light of the experience of persecution (Chapter VII) is, however, a new approach which could be justified on still other grounds than those mentioned in my treatment of it. The other distinctive feature of this estimate of Bunyan is found in the claim that he was in advance of most of his contemporaries in the Puritan movement because (contrary to common opinion) he was broad-minded enough to recognize that the Christian life need not, and indeed does not, conform to a single pattern.

To my wife I am indebted for the closing part

CHAPTER I

John Bunyan, Labourer, Answers the Justices

EARLY in January, 1661, the magistrates of
Bedfordshire met in Quarter Sessions in
the county town. Sir John Kelynge presided
and his colleagues were men of privileged station in county and in national life. One of the
men brought before them, described in his indictment as a labourer, was by trade a tinker, or,
as he and his father before him preferred to
say, a "brazier." The charge against this man
reads strangely in modern ears, but it had been
familiar enough a generation earlier and was
again to stand against many worthy men. John
Bunyan, of the town of Bedford, was indicted
for "devilishly and perniciously abstaining from
coming to church to hear divine service, and
for being a common upholder of several unlawful meetings and conventicles, to the great disturbance and distraction of the good subjects of
this kingdom, contrary to the laws of our sov-
ereign lord the King."

Hate-good. The trial of Faithful closely parallels the trial by Jeffreys of Algernon Sidney
in 1683. In striking contrast is the dignified
and constitutional trial of enemies of Mansoul
before Emmanuel in Bunyan's *Holy War*. The
scene in the *Pilgrim's Progress* is so evidently a
composite record drawn from Bunyan's own
recollections and from reminiscences of his fellow sufferers that we may quote extensively from
his allegory.

Then a convenient time being appointed, they
brought them forth to their trial in order to their
condemnation. When the time was come, they
were brought before their enemies and ar-
raigned. The judge's name was Lord Hate-
good. Their indictment was one and the same
in substance, though somewhat varying in
form; the contents whereof was this: that they
were enemies to, and disturbers of their trade:
that they had made commotions and divisions in
the town, and had won a party over to their own
most dangerous opinions, in contempt of the law
of their prince.

Then Faithful began to answer, That he had
only set himself against that which had set itself
against him that is higher than the highest. And
said he, As for disturbance, I make none, being
myself a man of peace. . . .

Then proclamation was made, that they that

had aught to say for their lord the king against the prisoner at the bar, should forthwith appear and give in their evidence. So there came in three witnesses, to wit, Envy, Superstition, and Pickthank. They were then asked, If they knew the prisoner at the bar? And what they had to say for their lord the king against him.

Then stood forth Envy, and said to this effect: My lords, I have known this man a long time, and will attest upon my oath before this honourable bench, That he is ——

Judge. Hold! give him his oath. So they sware him. Then he said: My lord, this man, notwithstanding his plausible name, is one of the vilest men in our country; he neither regardeth prince nor people, law nor custom; but doth all that he can to possess all men with certain of his disloyal notions, which he in the general calls principles of faith and holiness. And in particular, I heard him once affirm, That Christianity and the customs of our town of Vanity were diametrically opposite, and could not be reconciled. By which saying, my lord, he doth at once not only condemn all our laudable doings, but us in the doing of them.

Judge. Then did the judge say to him, Hast thou any more to say?

Envy. My lord, I could say much more, only I would not be tedious to the court. Yet if need be, when the other gentlemen have given in their evidence, rather than anything shall be wanting that will despatch him, I will enlarge my testi-

faith without the divine revelation of the will of
God: therefore, whatever is thrust into the worship of God that is not agreeable to divine revelation, cannot be done but by a human faith;
which faith will not be profitable to eternal
life.

(3) As to what Mr. Pickthank hath said, I
say (avoiding terms, as that I am said to rail,
and the like), That the prince of this town, with
all the rabblement of his attendants, by this gentleman named, are more fit for being in hell than
in this town and country: and so the Lord have
mercy upon me.

Then the judge called to the jury (who all
this while stood by, to hear and observe) : Gentlemen of the Jury, you see this man about whom
so great an uproar hath been made in this town:
you have also heard what these worthy gentlemen have witnessed against him; also you have
heard his reply and confession; It lieth now in
your breasts to hang him, or save his life; But
yet I think meet to instruct you into our law.

Lord Hate-good now expounds the laws of
Vanity Fair, which Bunyan borrows from Pha-
raoh, Nebuchadnezzar, and Darius.

Then went the jury out, whose names were,
Mr. Blind-man, Mr. No-good, Mr. Malice, Mr.
Love-lust, Mr. Live-loose, Mr. Heady, Mr.
High-mind, Mr. Enmity, Mr. Liar, Mr.

Cruelty, Mr. Hate-light, and Mr. Implacable, who everyone gave in his private verdict against him among themselves, and afterwards unanimously concluded to bring him in guilty before the judge. And first among themselves, Mr. Blind-man, the foreman, said, I see clearly that this man is an heretic. Then said Mr. No-good, Away with such a fellow from the earth. Ay, said Mr. Malice, for I hate the very looks of him. Then said Mr. Love-lust, I could never endure him. Nor I, said Mr. Live-loose, for he would always be condemning my way. Hang him, hang him, said Mr. Heady. A sorry scrub, said Mr. High-mind. My heart riseth against him, said Mr. Enmity. He is a rogue, said Mr. Liar. Hanging is too good for him, said Mr. Cruelty. Let's despatch him out of the way, said Mr. Hate-light. Then said Mr. Implacable, Might I have all the world given me, I could not be reconciled to him; therefore let us forthwith bring him in guilty of death. And so they did; therefore he was presently condemned, To be had from the place where he was, to the place from whence he came, and there to be put to the most cruel death that could be invented.

Before accepting the invitation of the royalists to return and ascend the throne, Charles had made a declaration at Breda promising consideration for tender consciences, with an assurance that none of his subjects should be disturbed in the exercise of liberty of opinion concerning religion so long as the peace of the kingdom was preserved. But Edward Hyde, later Lord Clarendon, had great influence with Charles and returned with him from exile determined to reestablish the Church of England in exclusive, undisputed, and uniformly recognized possession of the souls of Englishmen. A subservient Parliament passed a number of acts known collectively as the "Clarendon Code," all calculated to destroy the vigorous life of the sects. Independent congregations like that to which Bunyan belonged in Bedford, the Baptists, and the Quakers, especially suffered, for they could not conscientiously conform to the prescribed forms of worship and church government. The first of these acts had not been passed, however, when Bunyan was arrested. He was a victim of the zeal of a young squire, who took shelter behind an old statute of the reign of Elizabeth, which prescribed imprisonment for those who refused to worship in the parish church.

One day in November, 1660, John Bunyan had gone to a hamlet near Harlington, a dozen miles from Bedford, to hold a religious service in a secluded farm-house. Only a handful of people were there, for word had gone out that the squire, Francis Wingate of Harlington House, had issued a warrant. Advised of the danger, Bunyan refused to abandon his purpose. He firmly met the suggestion that he should. "By no means; I will not stir, neither will I have the meeting dismissed for this. Come, be of good cheer, let us not be daunted. Our cause is good, we need not be ashamed of it; to preach God's word is so good a work that we shall be well rewarded even if we suffer for it." He was one of the leaders of the independent congregation in Bedford and his gifts as a preacher had led his friends to send him here and there among neighbouring villages to exhort and teach such as would hear. He knew that his example would count for much, and he dare not run from danger. He opened the simple meeting with a prayer and then, with open Bible, prepared to expound a text, only to be stopped by a constable and one of Wingate's servants. A friend agreeing to produce him next day at Harlington House, he was given freedom overnight and then taken before Wingate. The best that can be said for the squire is that he probably believed that the "conventicle" Bunyan had been expecting to address was in reality a nest of sedition. But when the constable specifically cleared the preacher and his farmer friends of any such suspicion, saying that very few were present and that there was no sign of arms, Wingate was apparently too proud to acknowledge his error and dismiss the defendant, or else too sure of his new position of authority to suppose that he could be resisted. Froude is not correct in suggesting that Wingate had no choice but to send Bunyan to jail. Probably he "had an ancient grudge to feed," for his mother had been heavily fined for her royalist sympathies, actively expressed, during the Civil War.

The exchanges between these two men, who were both thirty-two at the time, brought Puritan and Cavalier face to face with a dramatic simplicity in the issues at stake. Why would not the tinker mind his own business? It is always hard for the Cavalier man of the world to understand the "meddling, reforming spirit" of the "self-appointed guardian of public morals," or to appreciate the vagaries of those who prefer an inner light to the regularly authorized channels of religious instruction. The preacher replied that he could follow his trade and at the same time, without confusion, instruct the people, lead them to forsake their sins, and exhort

them to follow Christ. Whereat Wingate lost
his temper and swore that he would "break the
neck of these meetings." With provoking calm
Bunyan was content to reply that it "might be
so."

It was useless for friends to offer surety for
Bunyan's silence pending trial at the Sessions.
He could not, he said, leave off speaking the
word of God. So to jail he must go. While
Wingate was out preparing the necessary document, in came the local vicar, his father-in-law,
"that old enemy of the truth, Dr. Lindall." The
encounter must have brought small comfort to
the old man. In the face of his taunting questions, in which again the voice of authority challenged the freedom of prophecy, Bunyan showed
his ability to quote Scripture as skilfully as the
vicar.

I told him that if I was minded, I could answer to any sober question put to me. He then
urged me again, how I could prove it lawful
for me to preach, with a great deal of confidence
of the victory. But at last, because he should
see that I could answer him if I listed, I cited
to him that in Peter, which saith, "As every
man hath received the gift, even so let him minister the same."

Ay, saith he, to whom is that spoken?

To whom, said I, why, to every man that hath received the gift from God. . . . . Not being willing to lose the day, he began again, and said:

Indeed, I do remember that I have read of one Alexander, a copper-smith, who did much oppose and disturb the apostles: (aiming it is like, at me, because I was a tinker).

To which I answered, that I also had read of very many priests and Pharisees, that had their hands in the blood of our Lord Jesus Christ.

Ay, saith he, and you are one of those Scribes and Pharisees, for you, with a pretence, make long prayers to devour widows' houses.

I answered that if he got no more by preaching and praying than I had done, he would not be so rich as he now was. But that scripture coming into my mind, Answer not a fool according to his folly, I was as sparing of my speech as I could without prejudice to truth.

It is easy to see that the clash of policies represented by these two men brought out the less admirable traits of both. Our sympathies will go to one or the other according as we are accustomed to prize most highly institutional order and stability of doctrine or prophetic freedom and variety in spiritual gifts.

On his way to jail friends met Bunyan and prevailed upon him to consider a proposal made by the magistrate that he should be released if he would only give certain assurances. Once more he was at Harlington House. This time one William Foster, Wingate's brother-in-law, tried with fair words to prevail on him to stop preaching. "A right Judas," is Bunyan's comment, justified by the fact that Foster soon became an important lay official of the diocese of Lincoln and of the archdeaconry of Bedford, in which office he proved merciless in the persecution of nonconformists.

There was the usual argument on the one side, to the effect that no man ought to preach Christ's gospel, but he who was sent forth by bishop and by parliament; and the usual and sufficient reply on the other, that a call from God and a fire in the soul could not be kept within the bounds of bishop's license or of the statutes at large. It was of little use to argue further. The time for words had gone by, the time for deeds and suffering had come. "Thus," says Bunyan, "we parted. And verily, as I was going forth of the doors, I had much ado to forbear saying to them that I carried the peace of God along with me. But I held my peace, and, blessed be the Lord, went away to prison with

15

God's comfort in my poor soul." (*John Bunyan,* J. Brown, pp. 144, 145.)

It was several weeks before Bunyan's examination (one can hardly say trial) by the justices, the climax of which we have already recorded in his own words. He had every reason to seek release from the county jail by compliance and compromise, but to the question why he did not go to church he replied that the Prayer Book was made by man and that the Bible enjoined him to "pray with the Spirit and with understanding, not with the Spirit and the Common Prayer Book." After an astounding remark by Sir John Kelynge that the Prayer Book had been "ever since the Apostles' time," another judge asked,

What do you count prayer? Do you think it is to say a few words over, before or among a people?

I said not so; for men might have many elegant or excellent words, and yet not pray at all; but when a man prayeth, he doth, through a sense of these things which he wants, which sense is begotten by the Spirit, pour out his heart before God through Christ; though his words be not so many and so excellent as others.

They said that was true.

16

I said this might be done without the Common Prayer Book.

Sir John next tried to twist the meaning of a text Bunyan quoted and to prove by it that every man should be content with his calling.

He said, Let me a little open that scripture to you. As every man hath received the gift; that is, said he, as every man hath received a trade, so let him follow it. If any man hath received a gift of tinkering, as thou hast done, let him follow his tinkering; and so other men their trades, and the divine his calling, etc.

Froude comments that Bunyan "was compelling the court to punish him, whether they wished it or not." If we leave out of account a common man's claim to simple justice and to the "free enjoyment of person and property, up to limits fixed by known law," the traditional privilege of the Englishman, Froude may be right. It was not long before the spirit of persecution found ample support in legislation, and these gentlemen were in the meantime merely silencing a contumacious upstart whose example and exhortation endangered their hope that ecclesiastical uniformity might serve the ends of political sovereignty.

17

Three months after his examination, the clerk of the court was sent to Bunyan to urge him to conform. Insurrections in London, wrongly identified by the government with nonconformist activities, had produced a nervousness in royalist circles. Bunyan knew that he was in serious danger of exile. But he could not surrender his principles. "The law had provided two ways of obeying—one to obey actively, and if he could not in conscience obey actively, then to suffer whatever penalty was inflicted upon him." He saw what was coming and was much concerned with the question how to endure a long and tedious imprisonment or how to face death, if that should be his portion. He saw that he must "pass sentence of death upon everything that can properly be called a thing of this life."

He had recently married a second wife. He had four young children, one of them blind.

I found myself a man encompassed with infirmities. The parting with my wife and poor children hath often been to me, in this place, as the pulling the flesh from my bones; and that not only because I am somewhat too fond of these mercies; but also because I should have often brought to my mind the many hardships,

miseries and wants that my poor family was like-
wise to meet with; *especially my poor blind
child,* who lay nearer my heart than all I had
beside. Oh, the thoughts of the hardships I
thought my blind one might go under, would
break my heart to pieces. Poor child, thought
I, what sorrow art thou like to have for thy portion in this world! Thou must be beaten, must
beg, suffer hunger, cold, nakedness, and a thousand calamities, though I cannot now endure the
wind shall blow upon thee! But yet, recalling
myself, thought I, I must venture you all with
God, though it goeth to the quick to leave you.
Oh, I saw in this condition I was as a man
who is pulling down his house upon the head
of his wife and children; yet, thought I, I must
do it, I must do it.

One more attempt, and a pathetic one, was
made to secure Bunyan's release. In April,
1661, at the coronation of Charles, a general
pardon was given prisoners awaiting trial. Had
Bunyan received justice he would have been set
free then. His wife had actually made a journey to London to plead for him, and a member
of the House of Lords had presented a petition
on his behalf. The justices were ordered to look
into the matter at the midsummer assizes. Twice
Elizabeth Bunyan petitioned the judges. Sir

Matthew Hale was kind to her, but Judge Twisden and Sir Henry Chester insisted he had been duly convicted and Hale could or would do nothing. Acting on the advice of a friendly sheriff, she made yet one more effort, making her way into the great chamber of the Swan Inn, "where the two judges and many justices and gentry of the county were in company together." The visitation of the justices was a great social occasion and it took desperate courage for a peasant woman to press through the throngs in the inn courtyard and to search among the fashionable squires who were drinking jovially together till she was face to face again with Sir Matthew Hale. "With abashed face and trembling heart" she pleaded that her husband had not been lawfully convicted. Twisden and Chester interrupted her, "It is recorded, woman, it is recorded, he is convicted." One of them said it would be better for Bunyan if he would follow his calling instead of running up and down preaching. "What is his calling?" asked Sir Matthew. "A tinker, my lord!" cried several. "Yes, and because he is a tinker and a poor man," replied Elizabeth, "therefore he is despised and cannot have justice." To the final angry taunt of Twisden, questioning the source of Bunyan's teaching, she had the courage to answer, "My lord, when the righteous Judge shall appear, it will be known that his doctrine is not the doctrine of the devil."

So Bunyan went to prison and, but for occasional liberties granted by lenient jailers, lay there twelve years, and once again it was proved that stone walls cannot imprison an active mind nor man's cruelty to man discourage a soul's loyalty to God.

CHAPTER II

England in Bunyan's Days

"Bunyan's life, continuing from 1628 to 1688, embraces the most revolutionary and stirring period in English history."—*Cheever.*

W E CANNOT tell the full story of that "stirring period" in which Bunyan lived,[1] but to understand the conflict between the two types we have seen ranged in irreconcilable opposition we must recall some of the events and conditions which explain the temper of the protagonists.

At the beginning of the seventeenth century James I came from Scotland to the throne of England. On his way south he received a petition from several hundred Puritan clergy asking that the toleration they had enjoyed under Elizabeth should be legalized and made secure. Only so, they urged, could a clergyman safely exercise any measure of liberty in ritual prac-

---

[1] G. M. Trevelyan's *England under the Stuarts* (1914) will be found an admirable guide to the political and social life of the period.

tice, as in simplifying the service, eliminating
Popish symbols, and encouraging preaching.
The petitioners also desired liberty to make
reservations in their assent to the doctrinal standards of the Church. At a conference at Hamp-
ton Court, James gave his support to the bishops
and angrily dismissed the petitioners with words
which revealed his sole concern in the discussion. "No bishop, no king. . . . If this be all
your party hath to say, I will make them conform themselves, or else will harry them out of
the land." Remembering what Puritan leaders
had demanded a generation earlier, their "policy and parity," as he put it, by which he meant
their desire for a Presbyterian form of church
government and for the parity of the clergy with
their bishops, he misjudged the Puritans before
him, mistakenly supposing he understood the
full significance of their requests. A royal proclamation soon appeared demanding complete
conformity from all the clergy. Three hundred
who refused were ejected (December, 1604).
Thus were added to the nonconformists already
outside the Church, Brownists and Separatists,
as early Congregationalists were called, an influential group of these "silenced brethren," who
promptly gathered about them willing hearers

and supporters. "Conventicles" were prohibited, but the result was one for which James had not looked. Meetings of nonconformists were given a domestic character. "The Englishman's house became his church, and his family his congregation." The practical concern of Puritanism for everyday life and its adoption of the vernacular of the cottage and the roadside may be traced to this enforced retreat of religion into the home.

The emigrations which in 1620 took overseas the Separatists, and a few years later the much larger numbers of Puritans, impoverished England but laid the foundations in the American colonies of a larger freedom than England was yet ready for. George Herbert could complacently urge the course of expediency, believing that

Though private prayer be a brave designe,
Yet publick hath more promises, more love,

and he could invite his readers to the comforts of conformity,

. . . let us move
Where it is warmest: leave thy six and seven:

Pray with the most, for where most pray is
    heaven.

But he could also see that persecution cost the
persecutor more than it cost its victim.

Religion alwaies sides with povertie.

.   .   .   .   .

We think we rob them, but we think amisse;
We are more poore, and they more rich by this.
Thou wilt revenge their quarell, making grace
To pay our debts, and leave our ancient place
To go to them.

    Bedfordshire was especially affected by Puri-
tan influences. In 1603 the vicar of Hawnes
was one of those who had waited on James when
he was a guest of the Cromwells at Hinchin-
brook to give him a "book of reasons" protesting against the use of the sign of the cross in
baptism, the prevailing lack of examination of
persons attending communion, the use of the title
priest for ministers, the "longsomeness of service, and the abuse of church songs and music,"
the profanation of the Lord's day, and the excesses of the archdeacon's commissary in dis-
ciplining people without the consent of their
pastors.

When Bunyan was a boy of six playing on the village green at Elstow, Archbishop Laud reported to Charles I, "My visitors"—he might have said inspectors—"found Bedfordshire most tainted of any part of the diocese." The nature of the taint we can estimate when we remember that Laud's arguments in support of the practice of bowing to the altar upon entering church were based upon the custom of the Order of the Garter, not upon any religious idea. "To him a church was not so much the temple of a living Spirit, as the palace of an invisible King." Records of the archdeacon's courts, which are in existence covering a period of many years prior to 1640, show that seemingly trivial offences and merely contemptuous behaviour were regarded by the ecclesiastical authorities, as probably by the guilty persons, in the light of gestures of disobedience. For "refusing to follow the cross in procession," for "hanging down the head at the elevation of the host," for "washing the hands in the baptismal font," for "singing the Litany derisively," for reading "heretical and English books" during mass, and for not receiving ashes on Ash Wednesday, men and women were fined and otherwise penalized. One man folded some sheep in a church during a

BUNYAN'S BIRTHPLACE AT ELSTOW, NEAR BEDFORD
From an old Print

snowstorm, another refused to have candles burning on the altar at his marriage, women came to church unveiled. Not all the offences, however, were of Puritanical intent. One clergyman so far forgot himself as to take upon himself "to the scandal of his calling, to be lord of misrule at Christmas among certain youngelings," while another neglected his duties to see an execution, and a parish clerk sang the psalms "with such a jesticulous tone and altitonant voyce, viz. sqeaking like a pigg, which doth not only interrupt the other voyces, but is altogether dissonant and disagreeing unto any musicall harmonie."

State papers of 1634 record the admission of Peter Bulkeley of Odell that "he never used the surplisse or the crosse in baptisme." This was the Peter Bulkeley who afterwards founded the Concord settlement in Massachusetts and was one of Emerson's ancestors.

In 1640 John Grewe, John Eston, and Anthony Harrington (who were ten years later to be among the founders of the Bedford Meeting) cited the vicar of St. Paul's, Bedford, for not administering communion to those who preferred not to come up to the chancel rail. In the following year, when Bunyan was twelve

and Strafford and Laud were lying in the Tower,
Sir John Burgoyne, with about two thousand
persons, including "the high sheriff, knights, esquires, gentlemen, ministers, freeholders and
others, inhabitants of the county of Bedford,"
rode four abreast through London and presented a memorial to the Parliament that was
resisting the will of Charles, congratulating the
members on their accomplishments, but asking
for the abolition of the Star Chamber and Court
of High Commission, protesting against the
votes of bishops in Parliament, and requesting
Parliament to provide a "learned, pious, and
conscientious ministry." Further indication of
the prominence of Bedfordshire in anti-royalist
activities is seen in the fact that of the eleven
"regicides" who were held responsible at the
Restoration for the death of Charles I two were
from that county.

The Civil War and the period of Commonwealth and Protectorate, whatever may have
been the limitations of Puritanism which they
revealed, changed the course of English history.
On the continent despotism was succeeding the
breakdown of the mediaeval system. In this
one country religious faith, expressed in a concern for the individual, sustained and directed

the political revolution. Cromwell, addressing
Parliament in 1663, spoke of the "strange wind-
ings and turnings of Providence, those very great
appearances of God, in crossing and thwarting
the purposes of men, that he might raise up a
poor and contemptible company of men, neither
versed in military affairs, nor having much natural propensity to them, even through the own-
ing of a principle of godliness and religion."
The great political issue of the age could be
as easily expressed, and was as widely discussed,
in terms of theology and metaphysics as in terms
of politics. The royalists welcomed any doctrine that would discredit Calvinism, with its
rigid faith in Predestination; for this reason
they found the Dutchman, Arminus, with his
doctrine of Free Will, congenial. So the victory of Arminianism would aid a coercive and
absolutist government and a sacramental religion, while Calvinism was synonymous with
the privileges of Parliament and the rights of
the individual. Richard Baxter served as a
chaplain in the Parliamentary army and tells
us that the "most frequent and vehement dis-
putes" among the soldiers were for liberty of
conscience, "that is that the civil government
has nothing to do to determine anything in mat-

ters of religion by constraint or restraint; but
that every man might not only hold, but preach
and do, in matters of religion, what he pleased."

When the reaction against the Protectorate,
which had been weakened by the death of Oliver Cromwell and the succession of his son Richard, brought Charles II to the throne in 1660,
the royalists had many old scores to pay off.
We have seen how promptly Francis Wingate,
for one, hastened to arrest a tinker who pre-
sumed to preach in the neighbourhood of his
demesne. The riot in London, led by Venner,
seemed to justify a proclamation from Whitehall restraining "all seditious meetings and conventicles under pretence of religious worship,
and forbidding any meetings for worship, except in parochial churches or chapels." Leading nonconformists disclaimed any connection
with the attempted insurrection, but in vain.
Parliament met in May, 1661, and Sir John
Kelynge was one of three to draw up an Act of
Uniformity. It was opposed as too rigorous but
finally passed in 1662, the votes being 186 for
and 180 against. The Lords reminded Charles
of his declaration at Breda about "tender consciences," but the king gave his assent to this
statute ordering every clergyman, before Au-

gust 24, to declare "publicly and solemnly" before the congregation his "unfeigned assent and consent to everything contained in the Book of Common Prayer." Either by coincidence or of set purpose this date was the anniversary of the St. Bartholomew's Day massacre of Protestants in France in 1572. Another clause made episcopal ordination indispensable. In all, two thousand gave up their benefices rather than comply. In spite of a declaration of "general religious toleration" by the king (in this yielding to Catholic advisers, who found uniformity as uncongenial as did the Independents, Baptists, and Quakers), Parliament passed a Conventicle Act in 1663. For the offence of being in a gathering of more than five persons for any religious purpose not in conformity with the Church of England the penalty was a fine of five pounds or imprisonment for three months. Further offences would be followed by deportation for seven years or a heavy fine. The Five Mile Act of 1665 banished the ejected ministers to not less than five miles from any city, town, or borough, or any place where they had formerly preached or taught. The prime movers in this legislation were Lord Clarendon, Archbishop Sheldon, and the Bishop of Salisbury.

William Foster, whom we met at Harlington House urging Bunyan to give up preaching, carried on a vigorous persecution as commissary of the Bedford archdeaconry, his victims being from various walks in life. Some are referred to in the records as esquires, gentlemen, or farmers, more are labourers, cordwainers, hempdressers, husbandmen, weavers, plow-wrights, fellmen, fullers, etc. After nine years of continuous persecution Archbishop Sheldon's inquiries revealed the fact that there were about a thousand nonconformists in the county.

A renewal of the Conventicle Act in 1670 was marked by fresh and yet more severe provisions. One third of the fine was to be given to the informer. The worst characters in the towns and villages were thus encouraged to climb trees so as to peep into houses and spy upon their neighbours at all hours. Power was given to justices to break down doors, and to lieutenants of counties to disperse assemblies with foot and horse. Resistance in Bedford was strong.[1]

James II, who succeeded Charles in 1685, wished to see the Roman Catholic church established and, with the purpose of winning non-

---

[1] Dr. Brown, in his *John Bunyan* (pp. 219, 220), gives interesting and amusing details of the encounters.

conformist support, made a Declaration of Indulgence in 1687. This annulled all the laws against nonconformists but at the same time it suspended the tests which had kept Roman Catholics out of office. Churchmen and constitutionalists were aroused and turned to the nonconformists whom they had lately despised to seek their aid in curbing the king. Dissenters thus actually held the balance of power. When the king tried to secure a Parliament sympathetic to his designs by remodelling the boroughs, he ordered the justices to find out how various men would vote if they were sent to Westminster. Our friend William Foster's reply is thus recorded, "He submits all to His Majestie's Pleasure." But Sir George Blundell, who had helped to send Bunyan to gaol, had learned how to resist dictation. He replied that he had no legal power to pre-engage himself before debate in Parliament, that he could not "pretend to a capacity of determining beforehand" what his thoughts and actions would be in the progress of time, and that he was sincerely willing to live peaceably with men of other persuasions, having no animosity to the person of any man for a difference of opinion.

The rebellions under Argyle and Monmouth

were followed by a reign of terror in which Colonel Kirke and Lord Jeffreys carried persecution beyond all limits observed before or since on English soil. Protestants of all shades joined hands to resist the foolish king. On the night of the acquittal of seven bishops, brought to trial on the king's orders because they had petitioned him against a further indulgence to Catholics, an invitation was sent to William of Orange to become king of England. The year of this bloodless revolution, which ushered in wider liberties and settled government in Church and State, was the year of Bunyan's death. From 1628, when men were presenting a petition of Right to Charles I, to 1688, when the last of the Stuarts was deposed, England had been a battleground of fundamental convictions and policies. In the struggle which thus covered the period of his life the tinker of Elstow and preacher of Bedford had played a worthy part.

Since the beginnings of the Christian Church there have been opposed to one another among the followers of Jesus in every generation two types of leadership. Each has claimed to be inspired by his example and his words and each believes that it perpetuates his purpose and his spirit. The one uses its talents in the creation

34

—and gives its energies to the maintenance—
of organized forms of procedure which, it believes, will best conserve the received tradition.
It cannot but dread, and it will not long tol-
erate, departures from the faith and the forms
which are supposed to have their authority in
historic fact. The other type of leadership is
that of men who find the prevailing forms of organization inadequate for the service of a chang-
ing society, who must find and use a vocabulary
of their own, who feel that they must claim
"liberty of prophesying" and that the word
given them to speak will lose its force if it waits
upon ecclesiastical sanction. These are men
who ignore customary times and places because
the urgency of their message makes them impatient of delay. Without doubting that God has
spoken "in former times," they are chiefly anx-
ious that men shall know the voice of the Living God who never leaves mankind without a
witness.

The opposition of these two types is the age-
old conflict between priest and prophet, of which
every religion has provided dramatic examples.
In seventeenth-century England the conflict represented not only divided opinion on religious

policy but also a far-reaching social opposition not unlike that which arrayed Amos against Amaziah and brought upon those that were "at ease in Zion" the denunciations of that herdman from the hills. The religious liberties which were won in that conflict were an anticipation and a guarantee of wider cultural liberties which later generations were to enjoy.

Puritanism is unfortunately remembered chiefly for its stern emphasis upon conceptions of morality uncongenial to modern minds. Schooled in the experience of persecution, it could itself be intolerant and use with little mercy the weapons of excommunication and intolerant scorn; it was ready at times to call down fire from heaven to destroy its critics, and quick to forbid those who would cast out devils by other formulae than its own. But George Herbert's picture of the conditions which called forth Puritan protest is not exaggerated.

O England, full of sinne, but most of sloth:
Spit out thy flegme, and fill thy breast with
     glorie.
Thy gentrie bleats, as if thy native cloth
Transfused a sheepishness into thy storie;
  Not that they are all so; but that the most
  Are gone to grasse, and in the pasture lost.

The Stuart court was notoriously corrupt, and, as Clarendon tells us, many noble families had already impoverished themselves with luxury and display before the Civil War completed or repaired their ruin. Drunkenness and coarseness of speech were unrestrained in Cavalier circles. The prosperity and relative freedom from war which was England's heritage from Tudor times provided the means and the justification for careless living. It was no disservice to English society that Puritanism raised a voice of rebuke and called men back to more lasting interests and concerns. But it is true that the protest was extended to sports and amusements innocent enough in themselves. Doubtless this was because they were often the occasion for excesses; it is hard for minds on the borders of fanaticism and bigotry to distinguish between occasions and causes. Further explanation for the Puritan's sweeping condemnations is found in his conviction that time commonly given to amusement might better be spent in the cultivation of piety. Miltonic theology and the precariousness of life in such an age helped to keep the thought of death and judgment before the minds of men who found few rewards for righteousness in this life and looked to another and a better world for their crowns of glory. Moreover, the Reformation had made the Bible a rule of faith and conduct and a literal interpretation seemed to support strict Sabbatarianism. Many old customs and festivities associated with Sunday and with special days of the ecclesiastical and secular calendars were condemned. We shall see that Bunyan suffered the tortures of a divided mind because his natural propensity to enjoy sports on the village green and to join in the merry bell-ringing at Elstow seemed vicious to him after he had been awakened to the claims of the more serious life of religion.

We must not forget that the extremes of Puritanism were in part a reaction against the ridicule levelled at religious people and those who were "righteous overmuch." In the *Pilgrim's Progress* Faithful tells Christian how he had met Shame on the way and how Shame enumerated the disadvantages of piety.

He said it was a pitiful, low, sneaking business for a man to mind religion; he said that a tender conscience was an unmanly thing; and that for a man to watch over his words and ways, so as to tie up himself from that hectoring liberty that the brave spirits of the times accustom them-

selves unto, would make him the ridicule of the
times. He objected also, That but few of the
mighty, rich, or wise were ever of my opinion;
nor any of them, before they were persuaded to
be fools, and to be of a voluntary fondness to
venture the loss of all, for nobody else knows
what. He moreover objected the base and low
estate and condition of those that were chiefly the
pilgrims of the times in which they lived; also
their ignorance and want of understanding in
all natural science. Yea, he did hold me to it
at that rate also, about a great many more things
than here I relate; as, that it was a shame to sit
whining and mourning under a sermon, and a
shame to come sighing and groaning home; that
it was a shame to ask my neighbour forgiveness
for petty faults, or to make restitution where I
had taken from any. He said also that religion
made a man grow strange to the great, because
of a few vices (which he called by finer names),
and made him own and respect the base, because
of the same religious fraternity. And is not this,
said he, a shame?

And what did you say to him?

Say! I could not tell what to say at first. Yea,
he put me so to it that my blood came up in my
face; even this Shame fetched it up, and had
almost beat me quite off. But at last I began to
consider, That "that which is highly esteemed
among men, is had in abomination with God."
And I thought again, This Shame tells me what

men are, but it tells me nothing what God, or
the Word of God is. And I thought, moreover,
That at the day of doom, we shall not be doomed
to death or life according to the hectoring spirits
of the world, but according to the wisdom and
law of the Highest. Therefore thought I, what
God says, is best—indeed is best though all the
men in the world are against it. . . .

But this Shame was a bold villain; I could
scarce shake him out of my company; yea, he
would be haunting of me, and continually whispering me in the ear, with some one or other of
the infirmities that attend religion: but at last
I told him, 'Twas but in vain to attempt further
in this business, for those things that he dis-
dained, in those did I see most glory: and so
at last I got past this importunate one.

We see from the records of the Bedford Meeting, which Bunyan joined after his conversion
and of which he became minister, how practical
a matter it was to make a religious profession
and to be a church member among the Puritans.
Brother Oliver Hicks of Milton, we read, lost a
sheep, and, a stray sheep being found in another
man's field, he was sent for "to owne if it were
his." He claimed it, and "tho' by the way (as
himself expressed) he judged in his conscience
that it was not his; yet did not carry it back

againe, but took it away and kept it, and sold the
fleece and would have sold the sheep." Brother
Hicks was brought before the justice and fined,
"all this to the great dishonour of God, the
wounding of his own soule, and a great scandall
to the Church of Christ, of which he is a member." Brought before the congregation, "after
a full debate . . . besides some confession of
his owne; his evill also being opened and
charged home upon him, he was by general consent withdrawne from for the present."

In 1671 Richard Deane was "cut off from and
cast out of" the congregation, charged with ungodly living and also with "defrauding in his
calling, selling to severall persons deceitful
goodes, to the great scandall of our profession."
John Rush was cast out "for being drunk after
a very beastly and filthy manner, that is above
the ordinary rate of drunkerds, for he could not
be carried home from the Swan to his owne
house without the help of no less than three
persons." Some were disciplined for running
into more debt "than they can satisfie, to the
great dishonour of God and scandall of religion." Sister Landy was admonished for
"countenancing Card-play, and for deceiving
the Church with her former seeming repent-

ance," Sister Maxey for "disobedience to her parents, to witt, calling her father lier, and for wicked carriages to her mother." Edward Dent of Gamlingay lost his membership for being negligent in the "management of his sister's Imployment . . . neither did he so honestly and Christianly take care to pay his creditors in due time as he ought." Mary ffosket was publicly rebuked "for receiveing and privatly whispering of an horrid scandal (without culler of truth)," and John Stanton for "abusing his wife and beateing hir often for very light matters." The record adds, "He seemed sory for his fault."

Puritans were not slow to point out the sins of others, but these selections from voluminous records show that with them holiness began at home. Indeed, a danger they did not escape was that of morbidity in introspection and self-reproach. Humanitarian concern for the needs of others and self-forgetful service played a small part in the Puritanism of the seventeenth century. We shall see, however, that in his later years Bunyan caught a glimpse of the social implications of his Christian faith.

Belief in the miraculous was almost universal and makes much of what Puritans wrote difficult reading to minds impatient with their "ignorance and want of understanding in all natural science." The only references Bunyan makes to his service as a soldier in the Civil War relate to two occasions when he was saved from peril, as he believed, by divine intervention. Once he fell into a "creek of the sea" (probably a ditch in the fen-country) and "hardly escaped drowning." On another occasion a fellow soldier took his turn at the last moment on a foray and was shot in the head. The consequences of divine intervention for the other man apparently presented no problem to Bunyan's mind. He was not displaying any unusual superstition. Cromwell, notifying Parliament of his successful retreat on one occasion, explained it by saying that "the Lord by His good Providence put a cloud over the moon." The *Pilgrim's Progress,* with its devils and angels, reflects the common thought of Bunyan's contemporaries, whose imaginations were provided with material from the writings of Milton and from sacred scriptures perpetuating primitive conceptions which are almost as old as the race.

We must remember that Puritans were not all of the same type, and we shall see that, contrary to general belief, Bunyan himself deliberately gave us several portraits of the Christian pilgrim. The principle which was central to Puritanism, the right of individual interpretation, inevitably encouraged individuality and involved the growth of sects, each arising out of loyalty to some one teacher and his doctrines. Milton and George Fox, Cromwell and Richard Baxter, Bunyan and Lord Fairfax, differing as they did, were alike products of the Puritan love of intellectual and civil liberty in union with religious fervor.

One distinction between Puritan and conformist must be briefly mentioned. As early as 1604, Archbishop Bancroft had persuaded James I that there ought to be a "praying" and not a "preaching ministry." "In a Church newly to be planted, preaching is most necessary, not so in one long established." The formalist "preferred catechising to preaching, and ritual to dogmatics; while the great body of indifferent and old-fashioned parsons . . . could only spell out the Prayer-book service, and then dismiss their congregations to keep Sunday round the May-pole." (G. M. Trevelyan, *England under the Stuarts,* pp. 170-171.)

Puritans, on the other hand, emphasized the exposition of Scripture and the application of its lessons. In "conventicles," as in Quaker meetings, the culminating moment was the free utterance of what the individual, learned or ignorant, believed to be communicated to him as divine truth by God's Spirit. It is to be noted that Bunyan's Pilgrim reaches the House of the Interpreter, a symbol of the experience of the illumination of the soul by the Holy Spirit, before he finds his way to the Palace Beautiful, which is Bunyan's symbol for the Church. In other words, prior to the benefits which come through Christian fellowship and before he is shown the "rarities" preserved by the Church ("records of the greatest antiquity . . . and the engines with which his servants had done wonderful things"), the pilgrim should have a personal experience of direct illumination. After the Interpreter has taken Christian through several rooms in his house he asks, "Hast thou considered all these things?" "Yes," answers Christian, "and they put me in hope and fear."

It is impossible to over-estimate the importance of this feature of Puritanism. To this day the dissenting or "Free" churches in England, and the communions elsewhere which have a similar origin in reaction against sacramentalism and authority vested in fallible human minds, cherish the prophetic ministry, even to the point of an undue disparagement of traditional procedure and orderliness in worship. They have had their reward in a close contact with the life of simple people. They have preserved the spirit that spoke in William Dell, of Yelden in Bedfordshire, of whom it was complained in 1660 that he had on the previous Christmas admitted one Bunyan, a tinker, into his pulpit, and that he had said he had "rather hear a plain country man speak in the Church that came from the plough than the best orthodox minister that was in the country." They have also all too often paid the penalty of separation from those ministries of beauty and comeliness in worship, without which even truth cannot for long be adequately mediated to the mind and heart.

CHAPTER III

A Tinker Tells How God Called Him

JOHN BUNYAN was born twelve years after the death of Shakespeare and three before the birth of Dryden. Milton was twenty and Richard Baxter thirteen. Dr. Brown's laborious researches into the history of the Bunyans (variously spelt Boynun, Boinun, Buniun, etc.) brought out interesting details which show that the family had come down in the world. In 1286 one of them "made service for half a knight." In 1327 another was living on the very spot at Harrowden, near Elstow, where John was born, and for at least eighty years before 1628 that end of Elstow parish was known as Bunyan's End. But in the middle of the sixteenth century a Thomas Bonyon was selling off piece after piece of his land. John's grandfather called himself in his will a "pettie chapman," which means a peddler of small goods. He was apparently not submissive to his superiors, for we find that he was haled before the court of the archdeacon's commissary in 1617 for telling the churchwardens that they were "forsworne men." Of John's father and mother we know little. In a memorandum book kept by the rector of the adjoining parish appears the jotting that "in Anno 1625 one Bonion of Elsto clyming of Rookes neasts in the Bery wood ffound 3 Rookes in a nest all white as milke and not a blacke fether on them." But we can hardly draw inferences from such scraps of information.

Bunyan has left us his own estimate of his family background.

For my descent, then, it was, as is well known by many, of a low and inconsiderable generation; my father's house being of that rank that is meanest and most despised of all the families of the land. Wherefore, I have not here, as others, to boast of noble blood or of any highborn state, according to the flesh; though, all things considered, I magnify the heavenly Majesty for that by this door he brought me into the world. . . . But notwithstanding the meanness and inconsiderableness of my parents, it pleased God to put into their hearts to put me to school to learn me both to read and to write; the which I also attained according to the rate of other poor men's children.

Growing up "among a company of poor coun-

trymen" he would hear many tales and see many
sights calculated to stimulate an already quick
imagination. His self-reproach for the childhood habit of lying we may certainly read as
an indication of his imaginative embellishment
of his experiences. He was subject as a child
and in youth to bad dreams which in keeping
with the superstitions of the age he attributed
to divine judgments.

My sins [he says] did so offend the Lord that
even in my childhood He did scare and affright
me with fearful dreams, and did terrify me with
dreadful visions. I have been in my bed greatly
afflicted while asleep, with apprehension of
devils and wicked spirits, who still, as I then
thought, laboured to draw me away with them,
of which I could never be rid. I was afflicted
with thoughts of the Day of Judgment night
and day, trembling at the thoughts of the fearful torments of hell fire.

The Bible was read in John's home as literally God's Word, and supplied him with vivid
pictures of a personal devil seeking whom he
might devour, angels and archangels in league
to save the souls of men from Satan's clutches,
and a personal Providence ordering for weal or
woe the details of every man's daily life. He

heard doddering old women cursed as witches, and as he went about helping his father mend pots and pans, or looked in at the door of the alehouse, he heard stories of strange ways in which, through sickness and mischances, God had brought blasphemous and wicked men to their doom. He tells us that in his youth he was "without God." But a dream he relates shows that his imagination was still busy on the theme of the moral government of the world and what God had in store for John Bunyan.

Once he dreamed [says a man who knew him well in his later years] that he saw the face of heaven as it were on fire, the firmament crackling and shivering with the noise of mighty thunder, and an archangel in the midst of heaven, sounding a trumpet, and a glorious throne was seated in the east, whereon sat One in brightness like the morning star. Upon which he, thinking it was the end of the world, fell upon his knees and said, "Oh, Lord, have mercy on me! What shall I do? The Day of Judgment is come and I am not prepared."

At another time "he dreamed that he was in a pleasant place jovial and rioting, when an earthquake rent the earth, out of which came bloody flames, and the figures of men tossed up in globes of fire, and falling down again with horrible cries and shrieks and execrations, while devils mingled among them, and laughed aloud at their torments. As he stood trembling, the earth sank under him, and a circle of flames embraced him. But when he fancied he was at the point to perish, One in shining white raiment descended and plucked him out of that dreadful place, while the devils cried after him to take him to the punishment which his sins had deserved. Yet he escaped the danger, and leaped for joy when he awoke and found it was a dream."

At the age of fifteen Bunyan lost his mother and less than a month later his sister Margaret. Before yet another month had passed his father married again. The effect upon a sensitive boy of this double loss, and of his father's unseemly ease in finding consolation, can be seen, perhaps, in the boy's abandonment to a careless life. This he later recorded in terms which his biographers have variously interpreted. In the light of his later convictions and evangelistic labours, it is not surprising that he should passionately reproach his youth with sinfulness. But when we look for any specific evidence of wildness, we note instead the pointed omission of any suggestion that drunkenness was one of his faults and the still more definite denial of unchastity. Probably he joined in youthful enterprises that involved a lack of respect for the property of others and entered into the sports of the village lads, all with a zest that kept his conscience busy in reproof while he succeeded in turning a deaf ear to its reproaches. He tells us that as a child he had few equals "in cursing, swearing, lying and blaspheming." His pride was hurt when, as a young man, he was rebuked by "a loose and ungodly wretch" who told him that "it made her tremble to hear him, that he was the ungodliest fellow for swearing ever she heard in all her life, and that it was enough to spoil all the youth in the whole town." It is true that confessions after the event are apt to exaggerate the sin confessed, and that careless speech may be a habit indicative of little but thoughtlessness, but it is also true that profanity may express a conscious irreverence which a man cannot but deplore when he is brought through a religious experience to attach a real meaning to the name of God.

The vigour of his "conviction of sin" when he finally chose another way of life cannot be taken as a proof of grave delinquency in his youth, but should rather be interpreted as a measure of the distance between his early indecision and his later resolution, a mark of his seriousness as a Christian rather than of the iniquity of his unregenerate condition. Dr. Brown, referring to Macaulay's defence of Bunyan against his self-reproach, takes Bunyan's words more literally. "We cannot read these easy-going utterances alongside Bunyan's burning words without feeling that these two men had gone through incommensurable experiences. Probably Macaulay's natural temperament and his career of unruffled prosperity led him to take a somewhat complacent view both of this world and of the next. Bunyan, on the contrary, had battled with the storm. He had looked down shudderingly into yawning depths and yearningly up to lofty heights, which when a man has once seen he can be complacent no more." (*John Bunyan,* pp. 58, 59.)

Bunyan went to the Civil War, probably among those drafted from his locality by the parliamentary leaders. Froude curiously argues that Bunyan served on the royalist side. His judgment is based on the fact that John Gifford, later (after his own conversion) Bunyan's pastor at Bedford, was a major in the royal army. But the two men never met till some years after the war! We have seen how strongly the county favored the parliamentary cause. The king's men there "had not any visible party, nor one fixed quarter" (Clarendon). Moreover, Bunyan was only sixteen when he went, and would hardly be so critical of the strong local influences of Puritanism as to go to another part of England to join the royalists. He may have been at the siege of Leicester in 1645, but apart from the "providential escapes" already mentioned [1] he gives us none of his experiences. He acquired, however, a great admiration for soldierly qualities, and this appears in more than one of the characters of the *Pilgrim's Progress.* Valiant-for-truth tells of his encounter with and victory over three highwaymen. Great-heart answers, "Thou hast worthily behaved thyself. Let me see thy sword." "So he showed it to him. When he had taken it in his hand, and looked thereon a while, he said, 'Ha, it is a right Jerusalem blade.' . . . Mr. Great-heart was delighted in him, for he loved one greatly that he found to be a man of his hands." Boanerges and Captain Credence, in the *Holy War,* are doubtless, as Macaulay says, portraits "of which the originals were among those martial saints who fought and expounded in Fairfax's army."

---

[1] Page 43.

INTERIOR OF BUNYAN'S COTTAGE AT ELSTOW

BUNYAN'S CHAIR, PRESERVED AT THE BUNYAN MEETING,
BEDFORD

Two or three years after his short war experience Bunyan màrried a woman of whom we know little. They were very poor, "not having so much household stuff as a dish or a spoon between us," John says. But she brought him memories of her godly father, of whom she spoke much, and also two books which helped, along with the responsibilities of marriage, to start serious reflections in his mind. One of these was *The Plain Man's Pathway to Heaven,* by Arthur Dent, an Essex clergyman. It was first published in 1601 and was so popular that by 1637 a twenty-fourth edition appeared. It is a record of a supposed dialogue, and while only a few racy passages approach Bunyan's own style, it doubtless helped to suggest to his mind as a picture of the Christian life the dangers and rewards of a journey over an unknown road. The other was *The Practice of Piety,* by Lewis Bayly, first published in 1612 and very frequently reprinted in the following fifty years. It was a great favourite with Puritans and was translated into other tongues.

The reading of these books and the influence of his young wife led Bunyan to begin going to the parish church "with the foremost." He felt a great reverence for everything pertaining to the church. "So overcome was I with the spirit of superstition that I adored, and that with great devotion, even all things (both the high place, priest, clerk, vestment-service, and what else) belonging to the church." Elstow church, it must be observed, maintained its episcopal forms without interference through the Commonwealth period, the clergyman being a Puritan and a compliant man.

No great disturbance, however, affected Bunyan's inner life as an accompaniment of this outward observance. He continued to join in the Sunday sports on Elstow green. Around the old stump of a cross, similar to many another in English villages, which may have been erected as early as the foundation of a Benedictine nunnery at Elstow in the twelfth century, young men played "tip-cat" (a forerunner of cricket) and danced away the holiday evenings with Jane and Joan.

Come lasses and lads get leave of your dads, and
      away to the Maypole hie,
For ev'ry fair has his sweetheart there, and the
    fiddler standing by,

   .   .   .   .   .

"You're out," says Dick. "Not I," says Nick,
  " 'twas the fiddler played it wrong."

56

" 'Tis true," says Hugh, and so says Sue, and
    so says everyone.

.   .   .   .   .

Then after an hour they went to a bow'r, and
    played for ale and cakes;
And kisses too, until they were due the lasses
    held the stakes.[1]

One day, as he played "cat," a voice seemed
to shout in his ear just as he was about to strike.
"A voice did suddenly dart from heaven into
my soul, which said, Wilt thou leave thy sins
and go to heaven, or have thy sins and go to
hell? At this I was put to an exceeding maze."
When he laid down the "cat" and looked up into
heaven it was as if he had "with the eyes of the
understanding seen the Lord Jesus" looking
down and "hotly displeased" with him.

He undertook an outward reformation, giving up swearing, to which he was prone, started
reading the Bible, and set about keeping the
Commandments. The result pleased him as
much as it surprised his old friends, and he took
considerable pride in his new condition. He had
been especially fond of the merry sport of bell-
ringing in the old bell-tower that stood beside

---

[1] From an old Derbyshire ballad, based on a yet older one
printed in 1672.

the church. He could not abandon it without a pang. His love of the bells remained through life and is noticeable at several points in the *Pilgrim's Progress,* as when Christian and Hopeful, approaching the Celestial City, "thought they heard all the bells therein ring to welcome them." He used to stand at the bell-tower door and watch others ring the changes, until he became afraid that this dalliance with sin might lead God to bring down the tower about his head. In a near-by village lightning actually did strike a church, pass through the belfry, and "trip up his heels that was tolling the bell, and strike him stark dead." Could a man want a more obvious warning? It was even harder to give up dancing and took him a whole year. At last, he tells us, he was able to say, "God cannot choose but be pleased with me."

Not yet was Bunyan brought face to face with the inward challenge of a religious faith. Had he been content with merely outward obedience he would never have given us, as he did in the *Pilgrim's Progress,* a scathing exposure of Mr. Legality and his son Mr. Civility, who lived in the town of Morality. Mr. Worldly Wiseman, who "looked like a gentleman," when he saw the dirt of the Slough of Despond on Christian and the burden that he carried on his back, told him his trouble came of "meddling with things too high" for him, and offered to direct him to what he desired "without the dangers that thou in this way wilt run thyself into" and to a place where he would "meet with much safety, friendship and content."

Christian. Pray, sir, open this secret to me.
Worldly Wiseman. Why, in yonder village (the village is named Morality) there dwells a gentleman, whose name is Legality, a very judicious man, and a man of a very good name, that has skill to help men off with such burdens as thine are, from their shoulders; yea, to my knowledge he hath done a great deal of good this way; ay, and besides, he hath skill to cure those that are somewhat crazed in their wits with their burdens. To him, as I said, thou mayest go, and be helped presently. His house is not quite a mile from this place, and if he should not be at home himself, he hath a pretty young man to his son, whose name is Civility, that can do it (to speak on) as well as the old gentleman himself; there, I say, thou mayest be eased of thy burden; and if thou art not minded to go back to thy former habitation, as indeed I would not wish thee, thou mayest send for thy wife and children to thee to this village, where there are houses now stand empty, one of which thou may-

est have at reasonable rates; provision is there
also cheap and good; and that which will make
thy life the more happy is, to be sure there thou
shalt live by honest neighbours, in credit and
good fashion.

Evangelist, reproving Christian for turning
aside from the way to go to the village of Morality, and after explaining what it was that had
befallen him when a high hill "did hang so
much over" that he was "afraid to venture further lest the hill should fall on his head," tells
him that Mr. Worldly Wiseman got his name
because he loved the doctrine of this world
which "saveth him from the Cross."

About this time, when Bunyan, who was himself "somewhat of a brisk talker on religion,"
was one day going to his work in Bedford he
overheard three or four poor women talking together as they sat in the sunshine in a doorway.
They were talking of such consolations and inward satisfactions of religious faith as he had
never known. They "spake as if joy did make
them speak," and with such an apt use of Scripture that he found himself in a new world. A
voice "darting into his soul from heaven" had
not done for him what the quiet, happy conver-

sation of these women was now to do. Again
and again he returned to learn from them of
the new birth to which they testified and of the
peace they had found. He was not to win a like
peace for himself without paying a great price.

CHAPTER IV

A Soul Divided Against Itself

"Grace Abounding should be read by any one who would learn why Bunyan became the prince of allegorists. The writer of this autobiography had lived the life of allegory. His soul was a battlefield across which contending armies fought."—*Samuel McChord Crothers.*

G*race Abounding* [1] is an extraordinary document. It has provoked the sneers of men who find in its pages the story of an experience remote from anything they have known, the grateful and enthusiastic endorsement of many others who, in following the alternations of despair and hope which it records, live through again their own anguished search for inward

---

[1] Grace Abounding to the chief of Sinners, or a brief and faithful Relation of the exceeding Mercy of God in Christ to his poor Servant John Bunyan; wherein is particularly shewed the manner of his Conversion, his sight and trouble for Sin, his dreadful Temptations, also how he despaired of God's Mercy, and how the Lord at length through Christ, did deliver him from all the Guilt and Terror that lay upon him; all which was written by his own Hand and now published for the support of the weak and tempted People of God (1666).

peace. It gives us only a few glimpses of the
man as he worked and went about amongst men,
but opens to public gaze the depths of a distracted and divided soul. It is not easy to read
it sympathetically to-day. One is inclined to
treat it as one might the objective record of a
psychopathic case. And, indeed, it is one of the
most important documents available, along with
the *Epistle to the Romans* (upon which it may
be said to be a commentary) and the *Confessions*
of St. Augustine, for the study of a certain type
of mental distress. Bunyan himself puts into
the mouth of Ignorance, when he "jangles with"
the pilgrims, the comment which he well knew
men of the world passed upon "enthusiasts" in
religion. "I believe that what both you, and all
the rest of you, say is but the fruit of distracted
brains." But the reality of the experience is
not affected by its classification and analysis.
Macaulay says that Bunyan was "made miserable by the conflict between his tastes and his
scruples." What such a misery may be, however, depends upon the character of the tastes
and the strength of the scruples. The issue has
been recorded as one between life and death.
"For I delight in the law of God after the inward man: but I see a different law in my mem-

bers, warring against the law of my mind, and bringing me into captivity under the law of sin which is in my members. O wretched man that I am! Who shall deliver me out of this body of death?"

The Puritan emphasis upon sin often found expression in what seem to us pathetic exaggerations of self-reproach. William Law, author of *A Serious Call to a Devout and Holy Life* (1729), wrote in his private papers, found after his death, with no intention of parading his feelings before the curious, "O my God, I am an unclean worm, a dead dog, a stinking carcass, justly removed from that society of saints who this day kneel about thine altar." Dr. Alexander Whyte, author of two volumes on *Bunyan Characters,* who quotes these words from Law, himself says, "How any man with a man's heart in his bosom for a single day can escape being the chief of sinners, and consequently the humblest of men for all the rest of his life on earth, passes my comprehension!" (Vol. ii, pp. 134, 135.) The world knew both as saintly men; they, however, knew the price of saintliness.

What he had heard from the lips of the "godly women," whose words had made "his heart shake," led Bunyan to seek out the company of pious people. His first experience was unfortunate. He fell in with a group of people called "Ranters," in technical language antinomians, who held that only those had attained perfection who could do as they pleased and yet not sin. He was tempted to follow the easy path which they claimed to be able to justify, but God "did not suffer" him "to accept such cursed principles."

Was he possessed of faith? He would test the point. Walking from Elstow to Bedford one day, he decided to command the pools on the road to dry up and went under the hedge to pray for power to work this miracle. But, just in time, he reflected that failure would only leave him in worse case and desisted!

A dream at this time anticipates his great allegory. He saw his pious friends of Bedford seated on the sunny side of a mountain, enjoying the sunlight and warmth while he shivered in darkness, cold, and mist. A wall separated him from these happy people and he found that there was but one very narrow doorway through which, painfully and laboriously, he had to make his way in order to join the saints. This vision showed him, he tells us, that no one can enter into life but those who are "in downright earnest," for "here was only room for body and soul, but not for body and soul and sin." Unhappily he could not believe he had made his way through this narrow entrance, so he found no comfort in the dream. Froude remarks, "a little comfortable self-conceit would have set him at rest." Perhaps, but there would have been no *Pilgrim's Progress.*

Next arose questions about his election; if God had not chosen him, all his effort was vain for "it is neither in him that willeth nor in him that runneth, but in God that sheweth mercy." He recalled a text full of comfort, "Look at the generations of old; did any ever trust in the Lord and was confounded?" He made a long search of the Bible to find these words and at last found them not in the canonical scriptures but in the Apocrypha, which Puritans disparaged as a menace to Protestant teaching. "Yet as this sentence was the sum and substance of many of the promises, it was my duty to take the comfort of it, and I bless God for that word for it was good to me. That word doth still oft-times shine before my face."

The good women had seen Bunyan's distress and had gone to their pastor, Mr. Gifford, to seek his aid. This man had had a strange career. He had been a major in the royalist forces and was taken prisoner in a severe engagement at Maidstone. As a notable man he was one of eleven condemned to death but, aided by his sister, he had escaped, lain three days in ditches, and made his way to London. Finally he found himself in Bedford, where he practised as a physician but "abode still very vile and debauched in life." One night, having lost heavily in gambling, he "thought many desperate thoughts against God," but something in a book he chanced to look into "brought him into a great sense of sin, wherein he continued for ye space of a moneth or above." He associated himself with the little group who maintained an Independent church at Bedford and during the five remaining years of his life "lost not the light of God's countenance, no, not for an hour, save only about two days before he died." He became their minister in 1653 and died in 1655.

Mr. Gifford counselled Bunyan, who became deeply attached to him and immortalized his help and guidance by portraying him as Evangelist in his allegory. Gifford, we learn from Bunyan, bade his congregation take special heed that they "took not up any truth upon trust, as from this or that, or any other man or men, but to cry mightily to God that He would convince" them of the reality thereof and set them down therein, "by His own Spirit, in the Holy Word."

But even with the counsel of John Gifford and the aid of Luther's *Commentary on the Epistle to the Galatians,* which of all books he ever read seemed to him "the most fit for a wounded conscience" and which certainly had much to do with the shaping of his religious ideas, Bunyan still had a long struggle before him. Probably Hopeful's list of things that brought his sins to mind reflects Bunyan's experience at this time.

Christian. What was it that brought your sins to mind again?

Hopeful. Many things; as:

    1. If I did but meet a good man in the streets; or,

    2. If I have heard any read in the Bible; or,

    3. If mine head did begin to ache; or,

    4. If I were told that some of my neighbours were sick; or,

    5. If I heard the bell toll for some that were dead; or,

    6. If I thought of dying myself; or,

    7. If I heard that sudden death happened to others;

8. But especially, when I thought of myself, that I must quickly come to judgment.

Two things, he tells us, made him wonder, "old people hunting after the things of this life, as if they should live here always," and professors of religion "cast down when they met with outward losses." Pitying them, he pitied himself the more. He was in even worse case. "My soul is dying, my soul is damning." He envied the rooks and the hares their brief, happy existence. His mind was tortured by thoughts of an infernal fire and all the "loathed variety of hell." Blasphemous suggestions haunted him, and he felt Satan's clutches in an almost physical way. When he prayed, the devil pulled at his clothes from behind and bade him stop.

The temptation to "sell Christ" affected him profoundly. "My very body would be put into action and motion, by way of pushing or thrusting with my hands or elbows." One morning, as he lay in bed assailed by this temptation, which he nowhere explains, he thought, "let him go if he will," and felt his heart "freely consent thereto." Then the battle was won, "down fell I, as a bird that is shot from the top of a tree, into a great guilt and fearful despair." Getting out of bed he went "moping into the field" where, for the space of two hours he was "like a man bereft of life." For many months he thought he had committed the unpardonable sin, and he fell into a condition of physical ill-health that matched his mental disorder. "Methought the very sun that shineth in the heavens did grudge to give me light." The curse he was under seemed to be written on everything he saw.

The Man in the Iron Cage of Despair at the House of the Interpreter is a detail Bunyan undoubtedly borrowed from his own experience. "I am now a man of despair, and am shut up in it, as in this iron cage. I cannot get out: Oh, now I cannot." The last words, "Oh, now I cannot," are taken verbatim from a book which helped to induce Bunyan's sad condition. It was, as Macaulay says, an "unseasonable addition to his library." It contained the story of a deathbed confession by Francis Spira, an Italian apostate, and describes how multitudes came to see him, many out of curiosity, others "to benefit themselves by a spectacle of misery and of the justice of God" in the ravings of a broken mind. Bunyan makes Evangelist quote from Hebrews

12:25, words which, Dr. Kelman says, "killed Spira and haunted Bunyan." These were, "if they escaped not who refused him that spake on earth, much more shall not we escape, if we turn away from him that speaketh from heaven."

Not without reason, again, is Christian made to say, in telling the story of Little-faith's encounter with three highwaymen, that the third rogue, who with one blow felled Little-faith to the ground "where he lay bleeding as one that would bleed to death," was named Guilt. "Oh! the unthought-of imaginations, frights, fears, and terrors, that are affected by a thorough application of guilt that is yielded to desperation." Vivid as are such descriptions in *Grace Abounding* of his struggles with devilish suggestions and nerve-racking fears, the immortal story the world knows best is that in which his pilgrim, Christian, is pictured at grips with Apollyon in the Valley of Humiliation.

Now the monster was hideous to behold: he was clothed with scales like a fish (and they are his pride); he had wings like a dragon, feet like a bear, and out of his belly came fire and smoke; and his mouth was as is the mouth of a lion. When he was come up to Christian, he beheld him with a disdainful countenance.

71

There is a wordy argument between the pilgrim and the monster, the conclusion of which is that Christian refuses to turn and go back and accept the wages Apollyon offers; instead he affirms again his allegiance to the King he prefers to serve.

Apollyon. Then Apollyon broke out into a grievous rage, saying, I am an enemy to this Prince; I hate his person, his laws, and people; I am come out on purpose to withstand thee.

Christian. Apollyon, beware of what you do, for I am in the King's highway, the way of holiness, therefore take heed to yourself.

Apollyon. Then Apollyon straddled quite over the whole breadth of the way, and said, I am void of fear in this matter, prepare thyself to die; for I swear by my infernal den thou shalt go no further; here will I spill thy soul.

And with that he threw a flaming dart at his breast, but Christian had a shield in his hand, with which he caught it, and so prevented the danger of that.

Then did Christian draw, for he saw 'twas time to stir him; and Apollyon as fast made at him, throwing darts as thick as hail; by the which, notwithstanding all that Christian could do to avoid it, Apollyon wounded him in his head, his hand and foot. This made Christian give a little back; Apollyon, therefore, followed his work amain, and Christian again took courage, and resisted as manfully as he could. This sore combat lasted for above half a day, even till Christian was almost quite spent. For you must know that Christian, by reason of his wounds, must needs grow weaker and weaker.

Then Apollyon, espying his opportunity, began to gather up close to Christian, and wrestling with him, gave him a dreadful fall; and with that Christian's sword flew out of his hand. Then said Apollyon, I am sure of thee now! And with that, he had almost pressed him to death, so that Christian began to despair of life. But as God would have it, while Apollyon was fetching of his last blow, whereby to make a full end of this good man, Christian nimbly reached out his hand for his sword, and caught it, saying, "rejoice not against me, O mine enemy! When I fall, I shall arise;" and with that gave him a deadly thrust, which made him give back, as one that had received his mortal wound. Christian perceiving that made at him again, saying, "Nay, in all these things we are more than conquerors." And with that Apollyon spread forth his dragon's wings and sped him away, that Christian saw him no more.

In this combat no man can imagine, unless he had seen and heard as I did, what yelling, and hideous roaring Apollyon made all the time of the fight—he spake like a dragon; and on the other side, what sighs and groans burst from Christian's heart. I never saw him all the while give so much as one pleasant look, till he perceived he had wounded Apollyon with his two-edged sword; then indeed he did smile, and look upward; but 'twas the dreadfullest sight that ever I saw.

Deliverance came to Bunyan at last. One day wonderfully sweet sounds came to him through the open window, whether of a gentle breeze or of angels' wings he could not tell, and a silence fell upon his heart to replace the "tumultuous thoughts" that had roared and bellowed "like masterless hell-hounds." Comfort came with the recollection of the text, "him that cometh to me I will in no wise cast out." For that blessed word he and Satan had striven. "He pulled, and I pulled, but, God be praised, I overcame him. I got sweetness from it. Oh! many a pull hath my heart had with Satan for this blessed sixth of John."

Never again was Bunyan oppressed by moods of melancholy. He awoke as from a troublesome dream, he tells us. But he could not dismiss this experience as insignificant. He took from it a virtue which was, as he puts it, like "honey from the carcass of a lion that once roared." He could almost cry, with another

Christian saint who also won his peace at great cost, *O felix culpa,* and bless the misery which had revealed the power and love of God.

He ever after had great sympathy for perplexed and fearful souls. He saw that wise guidance might have done for him even more than his good friends had been able to do. Perhaps he even saw, as we can surely see, that "many of the shapes with which he wrestled in deepest anguish were the phantoms of his own heated imagination, the result of his own misinterpretation of the book of God." He incorporated this hard-won wisdom into his immortal allegory to serve as a warning to others. Though Christian nearly sticks in the Slough of Despond, and Fearing struggles in it for a month, Faithful escapes the Slough altogether and has "sunshine all the way through" the Valley of Humiliation, "and also through the Valley of the Shadow of Death." Feeble-mind falls into the hands of Slay-good, but is rescued by Mr. Great-heart. Mr. Despondency, and his daughter, Much-afraid, were taken captive by Giant Despair in Doubting Castle, but they, too, owed their release to Great-heart, while old Mr. Honest cut down "at one blow" the giant's wife, Diffidence by name.

Yet the conviction remained with Bunyan that in some way God was fulfilling a good purpose in thus leading men through heaviness of spirit to peace.

Some must pipe and some must weep. Now Mr. Fearing was one that played upon this bass. He and his fellows found the sackbut, whose notes are more doleful than the notes of other music are; though indeed some say, the bass is the ground of music. And, for my part, I care not at all for that profession that begins not in heaviness of mind. The first string that the musician usually touches is the bass, when he intends to put all in tune. God also plays upon this string first, when he sets the soul in tune for himself. Only here was the imperfection in Mr. Fearing, he could play upon no other music but this, till towards his latter end.

Young James, Christiana's son, adds sententiously, "No fears, no grace. Though there is not always grace where there is the fear of God, yet to be sure there is no grace where there is no fear of God."

The Christian way of life, Bunyan had learned, is one that leads first to a Wicket-gate of decision. The Pilgrim meets Formalist and Hypocrisy, who had made a short cut ("what

they did they had custom for; and could produce, if need were, testimony that would witness
it for more than a thousand years"). It is to be
observed that it was only Christian, however,
who managed to surmount the Hill called Difficulty, while these two confident men ("if we get
into the Way, what's matter which way we get
in?") tried easier ways called Destruction and
Danger that only led in one case into a great
wood and in the other "into a wide field full of
dark mountains." It was the prevalent formalism and insincerity that called forth the Puritan
protest, and central to the Puritan emphasis upon
religious experience was this conviction that the
Christian must pass through a gate of costly
decision.

Another firm belief of the Puritan, to which
Bunyan gives vivid expression, was the conviction that on the Christian pilgrimage a man must
follow a way from which peril is never far removed. At the House of the Interpreter Christian hears a trembling man relate a vision of the
Judgment. "The bottomless pit opened, *just
whereabout I stood.*" Again, in the Valley of
the Shadow of Death, Christian was "put to it"
to keep the path. "When he sought in the dark
to shun the ditch on the one hand, he was ready

to tip over into the mire on the other," and "about the midst of the valley," the mouth of hell *"stood hard by the wayside."* Yet again, in Part II, Mercy asks the Shepherds at the Delectable Mountains, from which the Celestial City may be viewed, to allow her to look into "the hole in the hill that is commonly called the by-way to hell." This was evidently but a few steps from the pilgrims' way.

In 1653 Bunyan joined the church to which John Gifford ministered; he was the nineteenth to sign the roll, which had been kept from the foundation of the church in 1650. A year or two later, after the birth of his second child, he removed from Elstow to Bedford. He suffered poor health for a while, the result, doubtless, of the terrible strain he had undergone. Then his wife died, leaving him with four young children. About the time of the death of John Gifford in 1655, he was asked to speak in the meetings of the church, a request which did "dash and abash" his spirit. His hearers declared that they were both "affected and comforted," and he was called on to accompany various of the brethren as they visited villages and farms in the neighbourhood to preach and teach. Finally he was appointed more definitely to the work of preaching, though still in a lay capacity and without withdrawal from his occupation, much as Methodist lay-preachers still serve in English country districts. People came by hundreds and from all parts ("though upon sundry and divers accounts") to hear the tinker that had turned preacher.

CHAPTER V

Imprisonment Used to the Glory of God

FOR five years after his admission to the society of earnest men and women in Bedford, Bunyan spent much of his time preaching. His journeys, which give him a first-hand acquaintance with the dangers of travel and provided him with incidents for his allegory of pilgrimage, took him into adjacent counties, including Leicestershire and Cambridgeshire. He generally avoided disputatious matters and his message was a simple testimony to the deliverance he had found, followed by an appeal to his hearers to seek a similar victory over sin. His theology, derived largely from Luther's interpretations of Paul's epistles, was not speculative; his interest was in "the practick part" of religion, which he declared to be its soul. Utterance did not always come easily. Sometimes, after starting to speak with evident power, he would find himself at a loss for words or thoughts and then it seemed to him as if his head had "been in a bag all the time of the exercise." At times he suffered fits of nervousness and physical weakness, only to find in his unexpected success a great temptation to "pride and liftings up of heart." He laboured with great earnestness, however, and overcame these peculiar snares of his calling.

His work met with opposition and his right to preach was questioned. He was regarded as "a very pestilent schismatick." His qualifications, so satisfying to his Bedford friends, were not such as to commend him to the clergy and university men. Burton, who was his pastor after the death of Gifford, wrote of him once with evident reference to some comments upon his lack of learning, "This man is not chosen out of an earthly but out of the heavenly university, the Church of Christ. . . . He hath taken these three heavenly degrees, to wit, union with Christ, the anointing of the Spirit, and experiences of the temptations of Satan, which do more fit a man for that mighty work of preaching the Gospel than all university learning and degrees that can be had."

At a village not far from Cambridge a scholar from the university ("and none of the soberest of them neither") saw a crowd gather to listen to him. Learning who the preacher was, this college don gave a boy twopence to hold his horse, for he was "resolved to hear this tinker prate." In this case the result was unexpected, for the listener was led by what he heard that day to become a preacher himself. Another Cambridge man, whom he met on the road, asked Bunyan whether he knew the Scriptures in the original languages, and if not how he dared to preach. Bunyan was equal to this emergency. At another time, the university librarian heard Bunyan preach in a barn and challenged some of his statements. We may sympathize with his objection to Bunyan's sweeping declaration that most of his hearers, whom he had never seen before, were unbelievers. He challenged also Bunyan's right, as a layman authorized only by laymen, to preach at all. Dissatisfied with the answers he received, which were the rejoinder of a good debater but, as we might expect, not the considered arguments of a scholar, Smith wrote a pamphlet in extension of his criticism, warning his readers in conclusion of the "sad consequences to their souls, *bodies and estates*" and those of their children "in following such strangers." His phrases anticipate the coming

82

persecution, and many of Bunyan's hearers were soon to discover for themselves that their "bodies and estates" were indeed in danger if they preferred a wandering tinker to their parish priests. But there were those, even among the clergy, who defended Bunyan. William Dell, rector of Yelden, found himself in trouble for inviting Bunyan into his pulpit one Christmas day.

Along with preaching went pastoral labours which are recorded in the minutes kept by the church. These responsibilities included the rebuke of unworthy members of the congregation, consolation of the sad, and practical service of the needy. The record regarding John Rush, Sister Landy, and Sister Maxey already quoted [1] are in Bunyan's own handwriting.

When he turned aside in controversial effort he did less than justice both to himself and to his opponents. Particularly unfortunate was his severe criticism of Quakers, who were after all upholding the prophetic liberty so precious to himself. They emphasized the "inward light" and this seemed to Bunyan to involve a belittling of the Scripture. In him we see at work the process by which the greatest achievement of

[1] Page 41.

the Reformation was being undermined. The outward authority of a priestcraft had been overthrown, but the new liberty of private judgment was apparently too much for minds newly emancipated and the Scriptures were exalted till they occupied the place left vacant by the discredited rule of the Church. The followers of George Fox were contending, if Bunyan had only known it, for precisely that primacy of religious experience over outward forms and that emphasis upon individual responsibility of the soul to God which were so often his theme and so vividly brought home in his allegory. We need not follow him into the misunderstanding which separated him from men who could have taught him much, but merely note that his first ventures as an author were two books (*Some Gospel Truths Opened,* 1656, and *A Vindication of Gospel Truths Opened,* 1657) in which he takes his stand on the literal interpretation of the gospels as distinct from the mystical approach of the Quakers. His next book, *Sighs from Hell, or the Groans of a Damned Soul,* 1658, makes a literal use of the parable of the rich man and Lazarus. Its interest to-day lies in the promise it contains of the literary power to be displayed in Bunyan's more important writings. Following this came a work entitled *The Doctrines of the Law and Grace Unfolded,* 1659, a discussion of the person and work of Christ.

We now reach the year 1660, in which, it will be remembered, Charles II came to the throne. We saw that Bunyan was one of the earliest victims of restored royalist power. We followed him to Harlington House, we heard him some weeks later refuse before the justices to surrender his convictions, and we saw him go off to his prison "with God's comfort" in his soul.

For twelve years, with only a brief period of liberty at the end of the first six, Bunyan remained in prison without proper trial or review of his case. He was in the county jail of Bedford, which the great prison reformer, John Howard, described a hundred years later in his account of English prisons. A large oaken door, heavily barred, from the interior of this jail is still preserved in the Bunyan Meeting, as the church at Bedford is now called. There is no ground for supposing that Bunyan was ever in one of the two dungeons, and we know that he shared the common rooms with others. There were times when the prison was full of dissenters like himself and he held forth to them frequently. We need not suppose, with Froude, that Bunyan's imprisonment was at all a light matter. He once enjoyed occasional liberties for a short period, but his enemies heard of it and the jailer almost lost his position. After this his freedom "was more straitened than it was before" to the extent, as he puts it, that he could not "look out of the door."

What imprisonment meant to Bunyan may be judged from a trait revealed at many points in his writings but overlooked by his commentators. His moods were evidently largely dependent upon the weather. It is interesting to see in how many ways he shows us his love of the sunshine. He had noted that the "three or four godly women" who discoursed upon their religious experience in a Bedford doorway were sitting in the sun, and the dream which first suggested to him the wicket-gate through which a pilgrim must pass was of people seated "on the sunny side of a high mountain" refreshing themselves "with the pleasant beams of the sun" while he was "shivering and shrinking in the cold." His sad state during his long spiritual conflict was as if the very sun grudged him light, and the same suggestion is carried by the subtle touch introduced into his description of Giant Despair. In sunshiny weather the giant had fits, and then it was possible to overcome him. The birds in the groves about the House Beautiful, the Dreamer notes, "sing only in the spring when the sun shines warm." The distress that overtook the pilgrim in consequence of his sleep in the Arbour on Hill Difficulty was aggravated by the fact that the sun had gone down while he slept. In the Valley of the Shadow of Death he had an easier time when he came to the second part of the valley because the sun rose and "it was a mercy when the sun shone." In Part II of the allegory Feeble-mind finds the hospitality of Mr. Gaius "an unexpected favour and as the sun shining out of a very dark cloud," while we read of Mr. Fearing, who had spent a whole month in the Slough of Despond, that it was on a sunshiny morning that he at last ventured and so got over.

In his *Divine Emblems,* a book of verse written for boys and girls, Bunyan again reveals his feeling for the sunlight he must have missed so sadly in his prison. He speaks of "clouds edged with silver, as fine garments be," that

. . . look as if they saw the golden face
That makes black clouds most beautiful with
    grace.

and in another poem he welcomes the sunrise,
when brave Sol doth peep up from beneath . . .
"And gives us light to see our works and ways."
Of course he has a moral to point, but our purpose is served when we realize that these few
out of his many references to the warmth and
light of the sun are Bunyan's only complaint of
the dark and damp of his jail.

The friend who left us, in an appendix to
Grace Abounding, some details of Bunyan's life,
who was himself in jail when they met, tells us
that Bunyan did not "spend his time in supine
and careless manner, nor eat the Bread of Idle-
ness," but "ministered to his and his familie's
necessities making many hundred gross of long
Tagg'd laces to fill up the vacancies of his time."
Some of his sermons to fellow prisoners he ex-
panded into little books, such as *I will Pray with
the Spirit and with the Understanding also,*
1663, *Christian Behaviour,* 1663, and *The Holy
City* (an exposition of parts of *Revelation*) 1665.
The first of these, in addition to discussing
prayer, gives Bunyan's objections to the Book of

Common Prayer, which we saw him debating with Sir John Kelynge. A sense of sin and a fear of the wrath of God, he says, are a better prayer-book "than that which is taken out of the papistical mass-book, being the scraps and fragments of the devices of some popes, some friars, and I know not what."

Here now the wise men of our days are so well skilled that they have both the matter and the manner of their prayers at their finger-ends; setting such a prayer for such a day, and that twenty years before it comes, one for Christmas, another for Easter and six days after [? before] that . . . For each saint's day also they have them ready for generations yet unborn to say. . . . Look into the jails of England, and into the alehouses of the same; and I trow you will find those that plead for the spirit of prayer in the jail, and them that look after the form of men's inventions only in the alehouse.

Profitable Meditations, 1661, was a poetical dialogue between Satan and a tempted soul. As we shall see, Bunyan did write some verse worthy of comment, but not thus early. *Grace Abounding,* 1666, we have already used as a source of information in following his spiritual struggles prior to 1655. The second period of his imprisonment, which lasted from his short release in 1666 till 1672, saw the publication of only two books and these both late in the period.[1] The reason may well be that it was as dangerous for a publisher to bring his writings to light as it had been for him to preach; Milton's noble plea for the freedom of printing had not yet borne fruit. His silence from 1666 till 1671 was at any rate not due to depression of spirits. On the contrary, speaking of prison days, he says, "I never had in all my life so great an inlet into the Word of God as now. The Scriptures that I saw nothing in before are made in this place to shine upon me. . . . I never knew what it was for God to stand by me at all turns as I have found Him since I came in hither."

In 1672 the Declaration of Religious Indulgence, suspending all penal laws against non-

---

[1] (a) *A Defence of the Doctrine of Justification by Faith,* 1671, a controversial work criticizing *The Design of Christianity* by Edward Fowler, afterwards Bishop of Gloucester. He attributes to Fowler the view that we may wisely follow custom, our superiors, and convenience in matters of worship.

(b) *A Confession of Faith,* 1672, discussing baptism and its necessity as an ordinance. He has no sympathy with the rigid demands made by many Baptists of his day. "You must know I am still of that mind, and shall be so long as I see the effects that follow, viz., the breach of love taking off Christians from the more weighty things of God, and to make them quarrel and have heartburnings one against another."

conformists and Catholics, brought release to John Fenn, John Bunyan, John Dunn, Thomas Haynes, Simon Haynes, and George Farr, prisoners in the jail of Bedford convicted "for not conforming to the rights [sic] and ceremonyes of the Church of England, and for being at unlawful meetings." In May of that year Bunyan was licensed as a teacher according to the provisions of the Declaration.

CHARLES, etc. to all Mayors, Bailiffs, Constables, and others, Our Officers and Ministers, Civill and Military whom it may concerne Greeting. In Pursuance of our Declaration of the 15th. of March, 1671/2, Wee doe hereby permitt and licence John Bunyan to bee a Teacher of the Congregation allowed by Us in the House of Josias Roughed, Bedford, for the use of such as doe not conforme to the Church of England, who are of the Perswasion commonly called Congregationall. With further licence and permission to him the said John Bunyan to teach in any other place licenced by Us according to our said Declaration. Given at our Court at Whitehall the 9th. day of May in the 24th. yeare of our Reigne, 1672,

By his Maties command,
Arlington.

For three years Bunyan now enjoyed freedom
and he was able to exercise the pastoral office
to which, while he was still a prisoner in January, 1672, he had been chosen. The church minute reads as follows:

At a full Assembly of the Church at Bedford
the 21st. of the 10th. moneth [January 21, 1672]:
After much seeking God by prayer, and sober
conference formerly had the Congregation did
at this meeting with joynt consent (signifyed by
solemne lifting up of their hands) call forth and
appoint our brother John Bunyan to the pas-
torall office or eldership. And he accepting
thereof, gave up himself to serve Christ and his
Church in that charge; and received of the
Elders the right hand of fellowship.

The church bought from Josias Roughed (or
Ruffhead), for the sum of fifty pounds, an orchard containing a barn, and this barn served as
a meeting-place till 1707. Later buildings have
been erected on the same site. Bunyan applied
for licences for twenty-five other preachers and
for thirty other buildings (in Northamptonshire,
Buckinghamshire, and Hertfordshire, as well as
his own county) when he applied for his own.
The application, in Bunyan's handwriting, is in
the Record Office in London. His work now

took him far afield and he was a recognized leader of non-conformity. Some expository books and pamphlets came from his pen, but his chief work was preaching and the oversight of a congregation belonging not to Bedford only but also to widely-scattered villages.

His freedom was interrupted in 1675, when the recall of preachers' licences led to his imprisonment again, this time in a small jail, which was also a toll-house, built on a bridge over the Ouse. Here he was confined for only a few months, but they were the most significant of all he spent in prison, for he produced in 1676 (though it was not published till 1678) the great work which has carried his name around the world and which gave him his place as the prince of allegorists. The *Pilgrim's Progress* must now engage our attention. Perhaps, having followed its author through his spiritual struggles and through persecution and imprisonment, we shall be the better prepared to understand how such a work could spring from the brain of a village tinker.

CHAPTER VI

The Story of a Pilgrim Soul: I

Would'st read thyself, and read thou know'st not
what,
And yet know whether thou art blest or not,
By reading the same lines? O then come hither,
And lay my book, thy head, and heart, together.
The Author's Apology for his Book.

IN THE comparative quiet of the small prison
on Bedford Bridge, away from the excitement of frequent preaching, Bunyan told again
the story of his spiritual pilgrimage, but such
is the difference in tone and temper between
Grace Abounding and *Pilgrim's Progress* that
for every reader of the former there have been
hundreds of thousands of the latter. What is
the meaning of life? What is there to give significance to the vicissitudes of life? Whence
comes the authority of the demands which life
makes for courage, wisdom, truth? With such
questions great interpreters of life have dealt.
Their answers have been given to the world in

intellectual systems and formulas, in poetry, in drama, in architecture, in ritual and, much less often, in living embodiments of men's highest ideals. Each is marked and limited by features which show it to be a child of its age; each, if it be a truly great answer, has timeless elements to guarantee its service to other ages. That *Pilgrim's Progress* is a child of its age, in the sense that it speaks with complete sincerity the language of Puritanism, is true; those who know only the latest idiom of their own circle find this a barrier. Not that the actual words are hard to understand; on the contrary, though it contains many archaic expressions, it is so simple and direct that peasant people have known it by heart as they knew the Psalms of David and the Gospel parables. But only those who are willing to see the depth of Puritanism as well as its breadth, its lasting service to Protestantism as well as its exaggeration of an unlovely sternness and scorn of beauty, can discover the timeless truths of Bunyan's allegory.

To give a detailed account of a story so universally accessible, whose main features are so well known, is superfluous. A few characteristic passages, linked together by a bare outline of the story, will serve to recall to those who already know it the vivid characterizations and the combination of simplicity and subtlety which so largely account for its power.

As I walked through the wilderness of this world, I lighted on a certain place where was a den, and laid me down in that place to sleep; and as I slept, I dreamed a dream. I dreamed, and behold, I saw a man clothed with rags standing in a certain place, with his face from his own house, a book in his hand, and a great burden upon his back.

The Dreamer is Bunyan and the den is his jail. The book read by the man clothed in rags warns him of a judgment to come; the burden of his sins makes him fear. His friends think "some phrensy distemper" has got into his head and they drive him to solitary prayer and musing. In the fields he meets one named Evangelist, who represents the ministry. This figure was probably suggested by Bunyan's own pastor, Mr. Gifford, who had "expounded unto him the way of God." Evangelist advises the poor man to flee from the City of Destruction.

Then said Evangelist, If this be thy condition, why standest thou still? He answered, Because I know not whither to go. Then he gave

THE
Pilgrim's Progress
FROM
THIS WORLD,
TO

That which is to come:

Delivered under the Similitude of a

DREAM

Wherein is Difcovered,
The manner of his fetting out,
His Dangerous Journey; And fafe
Arrival at the Defired Countrey.

I have ufed Similitudes, Hof. 12. 10.

By *John Bunyan.*

Licenfed and Entred accozding to Ozder.

LONDON,
Printed for *Nath. Ponder* at the *Peacock*
in the *Poultrey* near *Cornhil,* 1678.

him a parchment roll, and there was written within, "Fly from the wrath to come."

The man therefore read it, and, looking upon Evangelist very carefully, said, Whither must I fly? Then said Evangelist (pointing with his finger over a very wide field), Do you see yonder wicket-gate? The man said, No. Then said the other, Do you see yonder shining light? He said, I think I do. Then said Evangelist, Keep that light in your eye, and go up directly thereto, so shalt thou see the gate; at which, when thou knockest, it shall be told thee what thou shalt do. So I saw in my dream that the man began to run.

Evangelist, it will be observed, cannot give the poor man complete directions, and the wicket-gate cannot yet be seen, but he can point him to a shining light and direct him to keep that light in his eyes. How often the minister's best service may be thus described!

Christian's wife and children plead; his neighbours mock and threaten; but he will not heed. There has been no more common criticism of Bunyan than that he makes his pilgrim ignore natural ties and the claims of family and friends to seek safety for himself. It must be admitted that Puritanism in various forms has often encouraged in the individual an unworthy concern for benefits, here or hereafter, which he may enjoy without regard for others. This fact has called forth vigorous statements of the half-truth which has thus been overlooked, that no man can be fully saved till all humanity be saved. But, this admitted, it must be remembered that Bunyan wrote in an age when the great issues raised by Puritanism inevitably divided many a man from his brother and estranged men who were neighbours. The word of Jesus that discipleship might mean leaving family and lands was literally understood because it was literally true. The cause of reality and sincerity in religious profession involved a definite choice. We may deplore such division of men into mutually exclusive groups when it engenders strife or kills the natural affections. It remains true, however, that the world owes its progress in ideals not to men who merely thought they could see a light, but to men who have been willing to step out alone to find and to pass through a wicket-gate.

Moreover, Bunyan at last left prison. Eight years after writing the story of Christian's departure he wrote a second part of the *Pilgrim's Progress* when he was living under more normal conditions. This tells how Christiana and her children made their journey and reached the Celestial City. The fact that Part II brings men and women of several types safely through the same journey that Christian had taken, though with different adventures, seems to show that Bunyan himself felt the limitations of the earlier story.

Further, the necessities of the allegory, it may be urged, involved the apparent separation of the pilgrim from his home surroundings, but those who read the story knew that the whole pilgrimage was accomplished while Christian worked at his forge or in his fields and that the Celestial City was reached without his going a mile from his birthplace.

Christian's first adventure was to fall into the Slough of Despond. Not without the friendly aid of another, called Help, did he emerge from this bog. Labourers of the King, he learns, have tried for above sixteen hundred years to mend that patch of ground and countless cart-loads of instructions have been devoted to it without success. Some good steps have been placed across it ("the promises") but in bad weather they are not seen and not all those who see them can walk upon them.

Christian next meets Mr. Worldly Wiseman

and is persuaded that there is an easier way of
escape, so he turns aside to visit the town of
Morality and to seek out Mr. Legality and
Civility, his son. This is, of course, the escape
provided by compliance with the letter of the
law and "a polite sense of propriety whose exact-
ness is prompted not by conscience but by fashion." (Kelman) He soon found he was in
danger of bringing the whole of Mount Sinai
on his head, and his burden became heavier.
Evangelist once more sets him on the way, with
suitable rebuke, and holds forth on the sin of
turning out of the way to escape the cross.

Then did Christian address himself to go
back; and Evangelist, after he had kissed him,
gave him one smile, and bid him God speed; so
he went on with haste, neither spake he to any
man by the way; nor, if any asked him, would
he vouchsafe them an answer. He went like
one that was all the while treading on forbidden
ground, and could by no means think himself
safe, till again he was got into the way which he
had left to follow Mr. Worldly Wiseman's
counsel; so in process of time, Christian got up
to the gate.

At the Wicket-gate, which might have been
named Decision, he learns that the way he is

to travel is narrow; thus, indeed, may he distinguish it from the many crooked and wide ways. He is directed to the House of the Interpreter, which stands for spiritual illumination, and there he is shown exhibits which put him in hope and fear.

Hope is kindled by the sight of grace at work in human hearts.

Then I saw in my dream, that the Interpreter took Christian by the hand, and led him into a place where was a fire burning against a wall, and one standing by it, always casting much water upon it to quench it; yet did the fire burn higher and hotter.

Then said Christian, What means this?

The Interpreter answered, This fire is the work of grace that is wrought in the heart; he that casts water upon it to extinguish and put it out is the devil: but in that thou seest the fire notwithstanding burn higher and hotter, thou shalt also see the reason of that. So he had him about to the other side of the wall, where he saw a man with a vessel of oil in his hand, of the which he did also continually cast (but secretly) into the fire.

Then said Christian, What means this?

The Interpreter answered, This is Christ, who continually, with the oil of his grace, maintains the work already begun in the heart; by the means of which, notwithstanding what the devil can do, the souls of his people prove gracious still. And in that thou sawest that the man stood behind the wall to maintain the fire; this is to teach thee, that it is hard for the tempted to see how this work of grace is maintained in the soul.

Fear, however, is stirred by the sight of the man imprisoned in the Iron Cage of Despair, who (as we have already seen) typified an experience Bunyan understood only too well.

The pilgrim goes on at a run and reaches a Cross, the mere sight of which loosed his burden. "Then was Christian glad and lightsome." Three Shining Ones prepare him for the rest of his journey and he goes on singing, clad in new raiment, carrying a roll to be read as he runs and to be presented at the gates of the City.

The hill called Difficulty slows him down.

I perceived he fell from running to going, and from going to clambering upon his hands and his knees, because of the steepness of the place. Now about the mid-way to the top of the hill was a pleasant arbour, made by the Lord of the hill for the refreshment of weary travellers. Thither, therefore, Christian got, where also he sat down to rest him: then he pulled his roll out of his bosom, and read therein to his comfort; he also now began afresh to take a review of the coat or garment that was given him as he stood by the cross. Thus pleasing himself awhile, he at last fell into a slumber, and thence into a fast sleep, which detained him in that place until it was almost night; and in his sleep his roll fell out of his hand. Now as he was sleeping, there came one to him, and awaked him, saying, "Go to the ant, thou sluggard; consider her ways and be wise." And with that Christian suddenly started up, and sped him on his way, and went apace till he came to the top of the hill.

The loss of his roll, his precious pass to the City, causes him much distress and he retraces his steps, finding it "down under the settle" on which he had slept. "But oh how nimbly now did he go up the rest of the hill! Yet, before he got up, the sun went down upon Christian; and this made him again recall the vanity of his sleeping to his remembrance."

The Palace Beautiful, which he next reaches, "stood just by the highway-side." It was suggested, some have thought, by the stately seat of the Earl of Ailesbury, Houghton House, at Ampthill, near Bedford. In the allegory it stands for the fellowship and encouragement

offered to pilgrims by the church. To reach it
Christian has to pass lions in the way, (civil and
ecclesiastical tyranny, perhaps) which he greatly
fears till the porter of the lodge assures him that
they are chained. "He heard them roar, but
they did him no harm." The Palace is carefully
guarded by Watchful the Porter, and by the
"grave and beautiful damsel, named Discre-
tion," who does not admit Christian till he has
told her whence he comes and whither he goes.
Entertained here by Prudence, Piety, and Charity—the last appropriately inquiring about his
family—he engages in profitable discourse before retiring to rest.

The pilgrim they laid in a large upper chamber, whose window opened towards the sun-
rising. The name of the chamber was Peace,
where he slept till break of day, and then he
awoke and sang,

Where am I now? Is this the love and care
Of Jesus, for the men that pilgrims are,
Thus to provide! That I should be forgiven,
And dwell already the next door to heaven?

So in the morning they all got up; and after
some more discourse, they told him that he
should not depart till they had shown him the
rarities of that place. And first they had him

into the study, where they showed him records of the greatest antiquity.

The next day he is shown the armoury and the equipment their Lord had provided for pilgrims, together with "some of the engines with which some of his servants had done wonderful things," Moses' rod, Gideon's pitchers, trumpets, and lamps, the jaw-bone Samson used, and David's sling and stone. Surely a humorous intent breaks through the allegory here as Bunyan recalls claims which were made by Catholics for relics and memorials of the saints.

Then I saw in my dream, that on the morrow he got up to go forwards, but they desired him to stay till the next day also; and then, said they, we will, if the day be clear, show you the Delectable Mountains; which, they said, would yet further add to his comfort, because they were nearer the desired haven than the place where at present he was; so he consented and stayed. When the morning was up, they had him to the top of the house, and bid him look south. So he did, and behold, at a great distance, he saw a most pleasant, mountainous country, beautified with woods, vineyards, fruits of all sorts, flowers also, with springs and fountains, very delectable to behold. Then he asked the name of the country. They said it was Immanuel's land; and it

is as common, said they, as this hill is, to and
for all the pilgrims.

True to his own and the common experience,
Bunyan brings his pilgrim promptly to the Valley of Humiliation after his happy and satisfying
stay at the Palace Beautiful. It was down-hill
going, and though he went "very warily" yet he
"caught a slip or two." In this valley he meets
and drives off Apollyon, monstrous embodiment
of inhuman temptations, in a conflict already related.[1]

The Valley of the Shadow of Death was a
region of vague fears and "discouraging clouds
of confusion" where the pilgrim must walk between a ditch and a "quag"; the mouth of hell
was "hard by the wayside."

Coming to a place where he thought he heard
a company of fiends coming forward to meet
him, he stopped, and began to muse what he had
best to do. Sometimes he had half a thought
to go back; then again he thought he might be
half way through the valley. He remembered
also, how he had already vanquished many a
danger; and that the danger of going back might
be much more than for to go forward. So he
resolved to go on; yet the fiends seemed to come

[1] See page 73.

nearer and nearer. But when they were come even almost at him, he cried out with a most vehement voice, I will walk in the strength of the Lord God. So they gave back, and came no farther.

The worst experience in this valley was to hear wicked suggestions, which, since he could not see the devils whispering them in his ear from behind, he "verily thought had proceeded from his own mind." At the end of the valley was a cave where dwelt two giants, Pope and Pagan, the marks of whose tyranny were seen in the bones and blood of men they had cruelly put to death. But the Dreamer tells us he had learned since his dream that—

Pagan has been dead many a day; and as for the other, though he be yet alive, he is, by reason of age, and also of the many shrewd brushes that he met with in his younger days, grown so crazy and stiff in his joints, that he can now do little more than sit in his cave's mouth, grinning at pilgrims as they go by, and biting his nails because he cannot come at them.

Now Christian falls in with Faithful and they go on "very lovingly together" exchanging ex-

periences. Faithful had escaped many of the
dangers Christian ran into and had had sunshine
through both the valleys his companion found
so terrifying. They converse with Talkative,
the son of Say-well, who dwelt in Prating Row,
in whom we have a picture of a type which was
the reproach of Puritanism. It took courage for
Bunyan thus to pillory men of his own side, but
no doubt he saw how just was the criticism they
aroused. Talkative offers to talk.

To talk of things that are good, to me is very
acceptable, with you, or with any other; and I
am glad that I have met with those that incline
to so good a work; for, to speak the truth, there
are but few who care thus to spend their time as
they are in their travels, but choose much rather
to be speaking of things to no profit; and this
hath been a trouble to me. . . .

Well, then, said Faithful, what is that one
thing that we shall at this time found our discourse upon?

What you will. I will talk of things heavenly,
or things earthly; things moral, or things
evangelical; things sacred, or things profane;
things past, or things to come; things foreign,
or things at home; things more essential, or
things circumstantial; provided that all be done
to our profit.

Vanity Fair, which the pilgrims at last reach, is a town in which a fair is kept all the year long. The way to the City leads through this fair, which was founded by Beelzebub to catch the pilgrims. Country fairs were familiar sights to Bunyan, and his description applies equally well to these and, allegorically, to the world and its vanities. A significant sentence tells us that "the ware of Rome and her merchandise is greatly promoted in this fair; only our English nation, with some others, have taken a dislike thereat."

The pilgrims caused a hubbub because, with their different raiment, they were regarded as "outlandish men" who spoke a language of their own (they and the men of the fair "seemed barbarians to each other"); and also because they spurned the wares offered them. They were examined by deputies of "the great one of the fair" and imprisoned in a cage. Their sober behaviour under persecution won to their side some of the inhabitants, but this only put the rest into a greater rage. Their trial by Lord Hate-good we have seen to be a reminiscence of Bunyan's own "trial." Faithful is put to death, but Christian, thanks to divine intervention, escapes and goes on his way. He has a new companion,

Hopeful, who has been moved by the sight of the pilgrims' constancy to throw in his lot with Christian. True to his name, he is sure that there are many in Vanity Fair who will "take their time and follow after." He is a wholesome influence, though his judgment is not of the best. There is a wealth of suggestion in Bunyan's selection of this man to be Christian's companion in the last stages of his pilgrimage. The problems of youth and early middle life are left behind; he is now at a point where a vision of the future and a hopeful bent of mind are his greatest need. We may leave the two to carry out their "brotherly covenant" and pause to consider one of the main motives of the allegory to which we have so far not referred.

CHAPTER VII

Interlude: The Motive of the Allegory

IN AGES of persecution a steadfast man who refuses safety when it is offered him at the price
of surrendered principles may hearten his fellow
sufferers by his example. If he is able also to
send to them from his prison written words
which renew their resolution, his service is even
greater and more lasting. He may have to conceal the heart of his message under metaphors
and parables, but his readers will understand.

Striking examples of works which are ob-
scure until this motive is discerned are the book
of Daniel in the Old Testament and Revelation
in the New. The one was addressed to the per-
secuted Jews who were resisting Antiochus Epi-
phanes about 170 B.C., to comfort them by recalling the loyalty of men who had been staunch
in the old days during the Chaldean persecution
and by promising the downfall of the vast Greek
empire and the defeat of God's enemies. The
other was occasioned by persecutions of Chris-

III

tians under the Romans and contained, beneath the disguise of cryptic numbers and strange figures of speech, promises of release from oppression and from the enforced worship of the emperor.

It does not seem to have been observed that Bunyan was guided by the same motive in his allegory, but once it is suspected evidence is found on almost every page. He is sending out his story at a time of renewed persecution when he himself, after the joy of what seemed like a final release on the occasion of the Declaration of Indulgence in 1672, is again in prison. Many had been deceived by the short lull in the storm and, supposing all danger over, had taken their ease, only to be caught unawares; others were now falling away in discouragement, the long years of strain having exhausted their reserves of loyalty and the rewards of faithfulness being apparently further away than ever.

The dangers of sleep (used, of course, as in the New Testament, to suggest the relaxation of vigilance) are reiterated throughout the story. It is when he sleeps in the arbour on the hill called Difficulty that Christian loses his roll. (In Part II Christiana at the same place forgets her "little bottle of spirits.") Simple, Sloth, and

Presumption are fast asleep in a hollow. The first when wakened said, "I see no danger." Sloth said, "Yet a little more sleep." In Part II Christiana found these three "hanged up in irons," and Great-heart explains that they had not only been foolish themselves but had persuaded Slow-pace, Short-wind, No-heart, Linger-after-lust, Sleepy-head, and a young woman, Dull, to turn out of the way and become as they. Even Mercy cries, "Let them hang, and their names rot, and their crimes live forever against them." In the grounds of Doubting Castle it is while they are asleep that Christian and Hopeful are caught by Giant Despair. And in telling the story of Little-faith Christian mentions that it was when he was awaking from sleep and not yet fully alert that he was attacked by the three highwaymen Faint-heart, Mistrust, and Guilt.

In the Interpreter's house Passion, who "will have all now," and Patience, who is "willing to wait," are shown to the pilgrim. At the hill Difficulty Timorous, who is on his way back, says, "The farther we go, the more danger we meet with; wherefore we turned, and are going back again," only to draw from Christian a brave word. "I must venture: to go back is nothing but death; to go forward is fear of death, and life everlasting beyond it: I will yet go forward." When Apollyon appears, Christian weighs the advantages of advance and retreat, deciding that as he has no armour for his back he may easily be pierced with darts and had better stand his ground. "For, thought he, had I no more in mine eye than the saving of my life, 'twould be the best way to stand." Apollyon taunts him with the common apostasy of pilgrims who profess allegiance to the King but "after a while give him the slip." Evangelist warns Christian and Faithful, before they reach Vanity Fair, that they will be "hardly beset with enemies," and that one of them will be called upon to seal his testimony with blood. "But when you are come to the town, and shall find fulfilled what here I have related, then remember your friend, and quit yourselves like men: and commit the keeping of your souls to God in well-doing, as unto a faithful Creator." Such words did not come amiss from Bunyan's pen. We recall him ready to face any penalty for preaching. "I told him . . . if I were out of prison to-day, I would preach the gospel again to-morrow, by the help of God." They ring true when they come from a man whose only fear of execution was lest he should "make a scrabbling shift to climb up the Ladder" and by "quakings or other symptoms of faintings give occasion to the enemy to reproach the way of God and his People for their timorousness." "Methought I was ashamed to die with tottering knees for such a cause as this." Bunyan had taken with him to prison two books, his Bible and a copy of Fox's *Book of Martyrs*. From the Quaker whose doctrines he had assailed he learned the joy of uncompromising witness.

The Declaration of Indulgence was received by dissenters with mixed feelings. Many, of course, welcomed relief from penalties, but there were those who saw it as a snare and a delusion. Mr. Love, speaking in the House of Commons in 1673, said, "I had much rather see the Dissenters suffer by the rigour of the law, though I suffer with them, than see all the laws of England trampled under the foot of the [royal] prerogative, as in this example." If liberty was to be theirs, they wished to have it by constitutional procedure. The royal clemency that could abrogate laws could all too easily become a royal tyranny. Perhaps it was this period of "indulgence" that Bunyan pictured in the Enchanted Ground. The air there "naturally tended to make one drowsy, if he came a stranger into it."

Christian will not listen to Hopeful's appeal for "one nap," and the latter sees his fault, admitting that he had "run the danger of death." We are told that the reasons for "sudden backsliding" are, first, that though the consciences of men are awakened their minds are not changed, so that when a sense of guilt wears away "that which provoketh men to be religious ceaseth"; secondly, that they have "slavish fears that do overmaster them"; and thirdly, that "the shame that attends religion lies also as a block in their way."

The manner of their backsliding is analysed in detail, and the passage is worth quoting as an evidence of the difficulty with which Puritanism had to contend.

1. They draw off their thoughts, all that they may, from the remembrance of God, death, and judgment to come.

2. Then they cast off by degrees private duties, as closet prayer, curbing their lusts, watching, sorrow for sin, and the like.

3. Then they shun the company of lively and warm Christians.

4. After that, they grow cold to public duty; as hearing, reading, godly conference, and the like.

5. They then begin to pick holes, as we say,

in the coats of some of the godly, and that devilishly, that they may have a seeming colour to
throw religion (for the sake of some infirmities
they have espied in them) behind their backs.

6. Then they begin to adhere to, and associate
themselves with, carnal, loose, and wanton men.

7. Then they give way to carnal and wanton
discourses in secret; and glad are they if they
can see such things in any that are counted honest, that they may the more boldly do it through
their example.

8. After this, they begin to play with little
sins openly.

9. And then, being hardened, they show themselves as they are. Thus, being launched again
into the gulf of misery, unless a miracle of grace
prevent it, they everlastingly perish in their own
deceivings.

Backsliders were among Bunyan's trials. In
Grace Abounding he tells us that if any of those
who were awakened by his ministrations fell
back ("as sometimes too many did"), their loss
was more to him than if his own children had
been going to the grave. "I think verily I may
speak it without any offence to the Lord, nothing
hath gone so near me as that."

By the time Part II of *Pilgrim's Progress* was
written, in 1684, the situation had changed some-

what. Christiana finds the Enchanted Ground now "all grown over with briers and thorns, excepting here and there was an enchanted arbour, upon which if a man sits . . . 'tis a question, say some, whether ever he shall rise or wake again in this world." It was "but sorry going" yet "they made a pretty good shift to wag along." The way was wearisome "through dirt and slabbiness." "Here, therefore, was grunting, and puffing, and sighing. While one tumbleth over a bush, another sticks fast in the dirt; and the children, some of them, lost their shoes in the mire. While one cries out, I am down; and another, Ho where are you? and a third, The bushes have got such fast hold on me, I think I cannot get away from them." We see that the story-teller sometimes gets the better of the moralist.

At a second arbour in this Enchanted Ground, "by the highway side," Heedless and Too-bold, wearied with their journey, are found asleep. "For when, thinks the enemy, will these fools be so desirous to sit down as when they are weary? And when so like to be weary as when almost at their journey's end?" (Did Bunyan know that the days of the Stuart régime were numbered?) "When heedless ones go on a pilgrimage, 'tis twenty to one but they are served thus."

Mr. Stand-fast, however, is found upon his knees, "with hands and eyes lift up," and Mr. Honest knows him at once; "he is certainly a right good pilgrim." We learn later that when he reaches the River of Death "there was a great calm at that time," and when he is half-way in he stands exhorting his friends, "This river has been a terror to many; yea, the thoughts of it have often frightened me. But now methinks I stand easy. . . . The waters, indeed, are to the palate bitter, and to the stomach cold; yet the thought of what I am going to, and of the conduct that waits for me on the other side, does lie as a glowing coal at my heart."

The theme of steadfastness inspired one of the very few memorable efforts of Bunyan to use verse-forms. It is found towards the close of Part II. It will fittingly close our study of Bunyan's motive in writing his great allegory of the pilgrim soul.

> Who would true valour see,
>   Let him come hither;
> One here will constant be,
>   Come wind, come weather.

There's no discouragement
Shall make him once relent
His first avow'd intent
   To be a pilgrim.

Whoso beset him round
   With dismal stories,
Do but themselves confound—
   His strength the more is.
No lion can him fright,
He'll with a giant fight,
But he will have a right
   To be a pilgrim.

Hobgoblin nor foul fiend,
   Can daunt his spirit;
He knows he at the end
   Shall life inherit.
Then fancies fly away;
He'll fear not what men say;
He'll labour night and day
   To be a pilgrim.

CHAPTER VIII

The Story of a Pilgrim Soul: II

WE LEFT Christian and Hopeful setting out from Vanity Fair. Their first encounter is with By-ends from the town of Fair-speech, who is related to Lord Turn-about, Lord Time-server, Mr. Facing-both-ways, and the parson, Mr. Two-tongues. By-ends had become a "gentleman of good quality" although his "great-grandfather was but a waterman, looking one way and rowing another." He professes a religion but it differs from that of "the stricter sort." He and his kind "never strive against wind and tide." The pilgrims, says By-ends, "after their headstrong manner, conclude that it is their duty to rush on their journey all weathers."

I am for waiting for wind and tide. They are for hazarding all for God at a clap; and I am for taking all advantages to secure my life and estate. They are for holding their notions, though all other men be against them; but I am for Religion in what, and so far as, the times and my safety will bear it. They are for Religion when in rags and contempt; but I am for him when he walks in his silver slippers, in the sunshine, and with applause.

Save-all, one of the friends of By-ends, brings against the pilgrims the charges that they are "righteous overmuch" and apt "to judge and condemn all but themselves," charges which Bunyan had doubtless heard directed against himself.

Bunyan's respect for the Church and its ministry at their best, revealed in his picture of the Palace Beautiful and his portrait of Evangelist, did not prevent him from making sly comments upon self-centered and worldly clergy. Mr. Money-love, another friend of By-ends, propounds an answer to the question whether a minister may legitimately increase his zeal in order to secure promotion.

Suppose a minister, a worthy man, possessed but of a very small benefice, and has in his eye a greater, more fat and plump by far; he has also now an opportunity of getting it, yet so as by being more studious, by preaching more frequently and zealously, and, because the temper of the people requires it, by altering of some of his principles; for my part, I see no reason why a man may not do this, provided he has a call, ay, and more a great deal besides, and yet be an honest man.   For why?

1. His desire of a greater benefice is lawful (this cannot be contradicted), since it is set before him by Providence; so then he may get it if he can, making no question for conscience sake.

2. Besides, his desire after that benefice makes him more studious, a more zealous preacher, etc., and so makes him a better man, yea, makes him better improve his parts, which is according to the mind of God.

3. Now, as for his complying with the temper of his people, by deserting, to serve them, some of his principles, this argueth, 1. That he is of a self-denying temper. 2. Of a sweet and winning deportment. And, 3. So more fit for the ministerial function.

4. I conclude, then, that a minister that changes a small for a great, should not, for so doing, be judged as covetous; but rather, since he is improved in his parts and industry thereby, be counted as one that pursues his call, and the opportunity put into his hand to do good.

Christian scorns such sophistry. "Even a babe in religion may answer ten thousand such questions. If it be unlawful to follow Christ for loaves, how much more abominable it is to make of him and religion a stalking-horse to get and enjoy the world."

A brief sojourn follows in "a delicate plain called Ease, where they went with much content," but this is so narrow that they quickly get over it ("the ease that pilgrims have is but little in this life") ; they have sight of Demas calling to pilgrims to visit his silver-mine in the hill called Lucre, to which, Christian sees, By-ends and his worldly companions "at the first beck" go over ; they are refreshed by a walk along the banks of a pleasant river and a sleep in a meadow "curiously beautified with lilies"; and then, the road becoming rough, they yield to the temptation to cross a stile into By-path Meadow, through which, as so often along English roads, a path follows the course of the highway and gives the pedestrian welcome relief from the hard, dusty surface. Night comes on while they are off the road and they must needs sleep in the field. They awake to find themselves in the power of Despair, a giant who lives in Doubting Castle with his wife Diffidence. He puts them into a dark dungeon, where they remain without food or light or a friendly word for several days. Their distress is so great that Despair suggests suicide, a counsel they reject on Scriptural grounds, fully expounded. Here it is Hopeful who offers comfort.

Who knows but that God, who made the world, may cause that Giant Despair may die; or that at some time or other he may forget to lock us in; or he may, in a short time, have another of his fits before us, and may lose the use of his limbs? And if ever that should come to pass again, for my part, I am resolved to pluck up the heart of a man, and to try my utmost to get from under his hand. I was a fool that I did not try to do it before. But, however, my brother, let us be patient, and endure a while; the time may come that may give us a happy release; but let us not be our own murderers. . . . My brother, said he, rememberest thou not how valiant thou hast been heretofore? Apollyon could not crush thee, nor could all that thou didst hear, or see, or feel in the Valley of the Shadow of Death. What hardship, terror, and amazement hast thou already gone through! and art thou now nothing but fears? Thou seest that I am in the dungeon with thee, a far weaker man by nature than thou art. Also this giant hath wounded me as well as thee, and hath also cut off the bread and water from my mouth, and with thee I mourn without the light. But let us exercise a little more patience. Remember how thou playedst the man at Vanity Fair, and was neither afraid of the chain nor cage, nor yet of bloody death: wherefore let us (at least to avoid the shame that it becomes not a Christian to be found in) bear up with patience as well as we can.

When Sunday comes they begin to pray and it is not long before their situation improves. Christian remembers a key called Promise that he carries in his bosom and they unlock door after door (the last lock "went damnable hard") till they regain the King's highway.

At the Delectable Mountains there are shepherds who entertain the pilgrims and allow them to look through a "perspective glass" toward the City they are seeking. Their hands shake at the remembrance of a by-way to hell which they have just been shown and they cannot look steadily, yet they think they see something like the gate, "and also some of the glory of the place."

From the neighbouring country of Conceit, by a little crooked lane, Ignorance joins them for a while, very confident that he will reach the City even though he has not entered the pilgrim way by the Wicket-gate. They see seven devils carrying off to hell a man whom Christian recognizes as Turn-away from the town of Apostasy, who bears on his back an inscription, "Wanton

Mountains delectable they now afcend,
Where Shepherds be, which to them do commend
Alluring things, and things that cautious are,
Pilgrims are fteddy kept by Faith and Fear.

CHRISTIAN AND HOPEFUL WELCOMED BY THE SHEPHERDS
AT THE DELECTABLE MOUNTAINS

A Woodcut from an Early Edition of Pilgrim's Progress

professor, and damnable apostate." This sight leads Christian to tell the story of Little-faith and his adventures with three highwaymen, Faint-heart, Mistrust, and Guilt. He and Hopeful next fall in with Atheist, who is coming in the opposite direction; for twenty years he has been looking for the City and has now made up his mind there is no such place. The Enchanted Ground now tempts the pilgrims to slumber, but "good discourse," in which we learn Hopeful's life-story, stands them in good stead. When Ignorance again comes up to them and "jangles with them," Christian has lengthy arguments to meet the man's confidence, but Ignorance regards all that he says as the "fruit of distracted brains." Temporary is discussed by Christian and Hopeful and provides the occasion, at the cost of the narrative-interest, for long discourses on the sin of back-sliding; these are happily interrupted by their arrival at the land of Beulah, where they solace themselves for a season.

Here they are in sight of the City and meet some of its inhabitants. They see the King's gardens, planted for his own delight and for the refreshment of pilgrims, and at length they are brought by guides to the river that lies between them and the gates of the City.

There was no bridge to go over; and the river was very deep. At the sight therefore of this river the pilgrims were much stunned; but the men that went with them said, You must go through or you cannot come at the gate.

The crossing of the pilgrims and their arrival at the City is described in one of the noblest and best-known passages in the whole story. We will allow the Dreamer to tell us how they fared, selecting paragraphs from what should be read without abridgment.

They then addressed themselves to the water, and entering, Christian began to sink, and, crying out to his good friend Hopeful, he said, I sink in deep waters; the billows go over my head, all his waves go over me. Selah.

Then said the other, Be of good cheer, my brother: I feel the bottom, and it is good. Then said Christian, Ah, my friend, the sorrows of death have compassed me about, I shall not see the land that flows with milk and honey. And with that a great darkness and horror fell upon Christian, so that he could not see before him. Also here he in a great measure lost his senses, so that he could neither remember nor orderly talk of any of those sweet refreshments that he had met with in the way of his pilgrimage. But all the words that he spoke still tended to discover that he had horror of mind, and heart-fears that he should die in that river, and never obtain entrance in at the gate. Here, also, as they that stood by perceived, he was much in the troublesome thoughts of the sins that he had committed, both since and before he began to be a pilgrim. It was also observed, that he was troubled with apparitions of hobgoblins and evil spirits; for ever and anon he would intimate so much by words.

Hopeful therefore here had much ado to keep his brother's head above water; yea, sometimes he would be quite gone down, and then, ere awhile, he would rise up again half dead. Hopeful also would endeavour to comfort him, saying, Brother, I see the gate, and men standing by to receive us; but Christian would answer, It is you, it is you they wait for; you have been hopeful ever since I knew you. And so have you, said he to Christian. Ah, brother (said he), surely if I was right he would now arise to help me; but for my sins he hath brought me into the snare, and hath left me. Then said Hopeful, My brother, you have quite forgot the text where it is said of the wicked, "There are no bands in their death, but their strength is firm; they are not troubled as other men, neither are they plagued like other men." These troubles and distresses that you go through in these waters are no sign that God hath forsaken you; but are sent to try you, whether you will call to mind that which heretofore you have received of his goodness, and live upon him in your distresses.

Then I saw in my dream, that Christian was in a muse awhile. To whom also Hopeful added these words, Be of good cheer, Jesus Christ maketh thee whole. And with that Christian brake out with a loud voice, Oh, I see him again; and he tells me, "When thou passest through the waters, I will be with thee; and through the rivers; they shall not overflow thee." Then they both took courage, and the enemy was after that as still as a stone, until they were gone over. Christian therefore presently found ground to stand upon, and so it followed that the rest of the river was but shallow. Thus they got over.

Now upon the bank of the river, on the other side, they saw the two shining men again, who there waited for them. Wherefore being come out of the river, they saluted them, saying, We are ministering spirits, sent forth to minister for those that shall be heirs of salvation. Thus they went along towards the gate. . . .

Now while they were thus drawing towards the gate, behold a company of the heavenly host came out to meet them; to whom it was said by the other two shining ones, These are the men that have loved our Lord, when they were in the world, and that have left all for his holy name; and he hath sent us to fetch them, and we have brought them thus far on their desired journey, that they may go in and look their

Redeemer in the face with joy. Then the heavenly host gave a great shout, saying, "Blessed are they that are called to the marriage-supper of the Lamb." There came out also at this time to meet them several of the King's trumpeters, clothed in white and shining raiment, who with melodious voices and loud made even the heavens to echo with their sound. Those trumpeters saluted Christian and his fellow with ten thousand welcomes from the world; and this they did with shouting and sound of trumpet. . . .

Now I saw in my dream that these two men went in at the gate; and, lo! as they entered, they were transfigured; and they had raiment put on that shone like gold. There were also that met them with harps and crowns, and gave them to them; the harps to praise withal, and the crowns in token of honour. Then I heard in my dream that all the bells in the City rang again for joy, and that it was said unto them, "Enter ye into the joy of our Lord." . . .

And after that they shut up the gates; which, when I had seen, I wished myself among them.

Would that we could end our account of the dream here! Bunyan unhappily does not. He adds an epilogue relating the arrival of Ignorance, who was helped across the river by a ferry-man called Vain-hope. He "came alone; neither did any man meet him with the least encouragement." When he looked at the writing above the gate he began to knock, but he could not produce his certificate. The King sent "the two shining ones" to take him and bind him hand and foot and have him away. He was carried through the air to that same door in the side of a hill which the shepherds had shown to Christian and Hopeful, and the Dreamer's last word is one of doom. "I saw that there was a way to hell, even from the gates of heaven, as well as from the City of Destruction."

"So I awoke and behold it was a dream."

CHAPTER IX

The Road to Ruin and the Battles of God
for Man's Soul

MANY to whom *Pilgrim's Progress* is familiar would be surprised to learn that Bunyan left between forty and fifty other published
works (including some that we should call
pamphlets) and that two of these, besides his
poetry, are imaginative in character. One is
wholly allegorical and the other may be called
fiction with a purpose. Of *The Holy War, or
the Losing and Taking again of the Town of
Mansoul,* Macaulay said that it would be the
greatest allegory in the language if *Pilgrim's
Progress* had not been written. Of the other,
The Life and Death of Mr. Badman, no one
could be as enthusiastic, though it is full of
interest to the student of Bunyan's thought and
language and of seventeenth century life.

Bunyan completed the third edition of *Pilgrim's Progress,* with several important additions, in 1678—three editions in the course of a

year testify to its popular appeal—and at once
set about the writing of what he evidently
planned as a companion but contrasting story.
As he had narrated the experiences of a victorious soul, so now he shows us a man going down
the road to ruin. Thus he defines his purpose:
"As I was considering with myself what I had
written concerning the progress of the Pilgrim
from this world to glory: and how it had been
acceptable to many in this nation: It came again
into my mind to write, as then of him that was
going to Heaven, so now of the Life and Death
of the Ungodly and of their travel from this
world to Hell." The book appeared in 1680.

The story is told in a dialogue between Mr.
Wiseman and Mr. Attentive. At the outset the
two are talking of the tolling of the bell on the
day before for a dying man, Badman by name.
He had never been anything but bad; even as a
child his lying, stealing and profanity troubled
his parents. He was so "addicted to lying that
his parents could not distinguish when he was
speaking the truth. He would invent, tell, and
stand to the lies which he invented, with such an
audacious face, that one might read in his very
countenance the symptoms of a hard and desperate heart. It was not the fault of his parents;

they were much dejected at the beginnings of their son; nor did he want counsel and correction, if that would have made him better; but all availed nothing." He hated Sundays and revealed his moral turpitude, according to Wiseman, by finding "reading Scriptures, godly conferences, and repeating of sermons and prayers" a trial to his busy mind and body. We are sorry for the lad—he was not the first nor the last to be severely judged by parents and observers who had forgotten their youth—and we should be inclined to say that he was misunderstood and mishandled. But Bunyan and his contemporaries saw original sin in every child and would have been surprised if they had been asked to take literally the great saying, "Of such is the kingdom of heaven."

The baffled father apprentices his boy to a godly master, who tries to influence his charge for good. But the boy robs the good man and runs away—as apprentices should in fiction. Now he is put under a master who proves to be as wicked as himself, but the young fellow's behaviour is too much even for this scoundrel and he has to be taken away and set up in business for himself. Bad companions bring him to bankruptcy, but his shrewdness enables him to

manage his affairs so as to come out of bankruptcy with enough money to start again while
his creditors carry his losses. He succeeds in
concealing his situation until he has married an
orphan who has large means. Her money goes
after his, and she finds herself deceived by his
glib professions of sympathy for her religious
zeal. After mistreating her brutally, he threatens
to turn informer and have her favourite minister
sent to jail. (We saw that the second Conventicle Act assigned a third of each fine levied under
its authority to the informer, and Puritan feeling was especially bitter against the spy. Badman's threat was the last indignity he could show
his wife.)

By cheating cutomers Badman becomes quite
prosperous. At this point in the story there is a
discussion of business ethics, indicative of the
concern of Puritan sentiment for the problem
of profits. Mr. Attentive opens the question.
"But you know that there is no settled price set
by God upon any commodity that is bought or
sold under the sun; but all things that we buy
and sell do ebb and flow as to price, like the
tide. How then shall a man of tender conscience
do, neither to wrong the seller, buyer, nor himself?" Mr. Wiseman's answer, if it were trans-

lated into terms of modern finance, would be revolutionary. "Let a man have conscience towards God, charity to his neighbours, and moderation in dealing. . . . Be sure that thou rememberest that thou knowest not the day of thy death. Guilt shall go with thee if thou hast gotten thy substance dishonestly, and they to whom thou shalt leave it shall receive it to their hurt. These things considered, I will shew thee how thou should'st live in the practical part of this art. Art thou to buy or sell? If thou sellest, do not commend. If thou buyest, do not dispraise any otherwise but to give the thing that thou hast to do with its just value and worth. *Art thou a seller, and do things grow cheap? Set not thy hand to hold them up higher. Art thou a buyer, and do things grow dear? Use no cunning or deceitful language to pull them down.*"

In a drunken revel Badman breaks his leg. While danger lasts he is penitent. "You would not think how he swore at frst. Then, coming to himself, and finding he was badly hurt, he cried out, after the manner of such, Lord, help me! Lord, have mercy on me! Good God, deliver me! and the like." But the mood wears off when he is about again. Several stories of judgments upon drunkards and blasphemers are introduced; they are typical of the superstition of the age. One will suffice as an example. "There was one at Salisbury drinking and carousing at a tavern and he drank a health to the devil, saying that if the devil would not come and pledge him, he could not believe there was either God or devil. Whereupon his companions, stricken with fear, hastened out of the room; and presently after, hearing a hideous noise and smelling a stinking savour, the vintner ran into the chamber, and coming in he missed his guest, and found the window broken, the iron bars in it bowed and all bloody, but the man was never heard of afterwards."

After the death of his wife, Badman marries again, this time a worthless woman; they are wretched together and they part at last "as poor as howlets." At last Badman himself dies in miserable poverty and still impenitent. Bunyan was artist enough to avoid a melodramatic ending, and he tells us himself that he is no admirer of sick-bed repentance. "I think verily it is seldom good for anything." Badman died "like a lamb, or, as men call it, like a chrisom child, quietly and without fear." A quiet death is no sign, Bunyan assures us, that a man is saved. On the contrary, there is "no surer sign of a man's damnation than to die quietly after a sinful life —than to sin and die with a heart that cannot repent."

Froude's judgment on the book is that "it is extremely interesting, merely as a picture of vulgar English life in a provincial town, such as Bedford was when Bunyan was there." It is certainly a mine of information for those who find it worth while to see just how, with the breadth of human interest and the depth of Puritan feeling that made Bunyan what he was, so representative a Puritan viewed those aspects of life from which he and his kind had so completely severed themselves.

The Holy War (1682) relates the plots of Diabolus and his friends (Apollyon, Allecto, Beelzebub, Legion, and others) to take the town of Mansoul; their success and their rule in the town; its recapture for Shaddai the King by his Son, Immanuel, who remodels it and provides a better government; and the putting down of further revolts. Shaddai (Hebrew, All-Sufficient, a name for God) had "made it the mirror and glory of all that he made."

The story is vivid, with many passages that

Bunyan could hardly have written had he not recalled in great detail what he saw and heard of war as a young man at the siege of Leicester and elsewhere. The allegory is consistently maintained and every detail is subordinated to its purpose. Given the conception of God's dealings with man which was Bunyan's starting-point, together with the idea of Satan and his operations in man's heart which was taken for granted by his readers, the allegory is a quite remarkable presentation of the "scheme of salvation" which Bunyan so largely helped to popularize as the framework of Protestant doctrine during the next two hundred years.

Diabolus and his plotters listen to the advice of Legion. "Let us assault them in all pretended fairness; covering our intentions with all manner of lies, flatteries, delusive words; feigning things that will never be, and promising that to them which they shall never find. This is the way to win Mansoul, and to make them willingly open their gates to us: yea, and desire us also to come into them. Now, the reason why I think that this project will do, is because the people of Mansoul are now every one simple and innocent; all honest and true; nor do they as yet know what it is to be assaulted with fraud, guile, and hypocrisy."

Diabolus draws up his army at the Ear-gate of the city—other gates are Eye-gate, Mouth-gate, Nose-gate, and Feel-gate—and addresses the people, concluding with an appeal to their pride. "Why should you not be enlarged in knowledge and understanding? . . . Ye are not a free people; ye are kept both in bondage and slavery, and that by a grievous threat, no reason being annexed. . . . And is it not grievous to think on, that that very thing you are forbidden to do, might you but do it, would yield you both wisdom and honor? For then your eyes will be opened, and you shall be as gods. . . . Will not reason tell you that it is better to have eyes, than to be without them?"

While Diabolus makes his speech, Captain Resistance—the only man of war in the town— is treacherously shot down; and when Ill-pause follows with further oratory "My Lord Innocency (whether by a shot from the camp of the giant, or some qualm that suddenly took him, or whether by the breath of that treacherous villain, old Ill-pause, for so I am apt to think) sank down in the place where he stood, nor could be brought to life again." Diabolus is admitted to the town and made king. He promptly builds a high wall before the house of the lord mayor, Mr. Understanding, to darken it, and appoints one of his own men, Mr. Incredulity, in his place. He feared the town recorder, Mr. Conscience, more than any other that was left alive in Mansoul because "his words did shake the whole town; they were like the rattling of thunder, and also like thunder-claps; since therefore the giant could not make him wholly his own, what doth he do but studies all that he could to debauch the old gentleman, and by debauchery to stupefy his mind, and more harden his heart in the ways of vanity. And as he attempted, so he accomplished his design; he debauched the man, and by little and little so drew him into sin and wickedness, that at last he was . . . past all conscience of sin. And this was the farthest Diabolus could go. Wherefore he bethinks him of another project, and that was to persuade the men of the town that Mr. Recorder was mad, and so not to be regarded. And for this he urged his fits, and said, If he be himself, why doth he not do thus always? But, quoth he, all mad folks have their fits, and in them raving language; so hath this old and doating gentleman. Thus by one means or other he quickly got Mansoul to slight, neglect, and despise whatever Mr. Recorder could say." [1]

When Shaddai learns of the revolution he and Immanuel agree that at a later time the latter shall "take a journey into the country of Universe, and there in a way of justice and equity, by making amends for the follies of Mansoul, he should lay the foundation of her perfect deliverance from Diabolus and from his tyranny."

First an army is sent out, which consists of "above forty thousand, all true men . . . under the conduct of four stout generals; Captains Boanerges, Conviction, Judgment, and Execution. When the army encamps close to Mansoul the people go out to gaze at the brilliant accoutrements, which angers Diabolus. "Gentlemen," says he, "although you are my trusty and well-beloved friends, yet I cannot but (a

---

[1] It is interesting to note that the very year in which Bunyan was writing *The Holy War,* 1681, a year of reaction and of reverses for dissenters, was one in which Charles succeeded in remodelling many of the boroughs so that municipal officers should be men favourable to the royal policy, and that in Bedford the first official made a victim of this unconstitutional procedure was the Recorder, Mr. Audley, who was friendly toward the dissenters though of the opposite party. Not long afterward seventy-six new burgesses were "elected," all of them King's men. Thus Charles secured control of the corporation of Bedford.

little) chide you for your late uncircumspect action, in going out to gaze on that great and mighty force that but yesterday sat down before the famous town of Mansoul. . . . Wherefore did you not rather, even at the first appearance of them, cry out, Fire the beacons, and give the whole town an alarm concerning them! Then had you showed yourselves men to my liking, whereas by what you have done, you have made me half afraid that when they and we shall come to push a pike, I shall find that you want courage to stand it out any longer. . . . Fie, fie, put yourselves in a posture of defence, beat up the drum, gather together in warlike manner."

At the Ear-gate, we read, an angry and ill-conditioned old fellow had been stationed as captain of the ward. This was Mr. Prejudice, and he had sixty deaf men with him! Another subtle touch is seen in the statement that "the King's captains . . . as they came crossing the country, happened to light upon three young men that had a mind to go for soldiers; proper men they were, and men of courage (and skill) to appearance." These were Mr. Tradition, Mr. Human Wisdom, and Mr. Man's Invention. Their services were accepted, but in a brisk skirmish they were taken prisoners by

Diabolonians and readily transferred their service to their captors. "They told him, that they did not so much live by religion, as by the fates of fortune; and that, since his lordship was willing to entertain them, they should be willing to serve him." The first two were made sergeants and the last an armour-bearer.

Famine and distress in Mansoul led some to grow restless. "New thoughts, and thoughts that began to run counter one to another by degrees possessed the minds of the men of the town of Mansoul. Some would say, There is no living thus. Others would then reply, This will be over shortly. Then would a third stand up and answer, Let us turn to King Shaddai, and so put an end to all these troubles. And a fourth would come in with a fair speech, saying, I doubt he will not receive us." There is complaint because Mr. Understanding and Mr. Conscience were not called to take part in a parley that was held with the King's captains, and these former officers of the town are promptly "clapped up in prison as the ringleaders and managers of this most heavy rioting." An appeal to Shaddai from his officers leads him to send Immanuel with a great army under five noble captains, Credence, Good

Hope, Charity, Innocent, and Patience. Each
has an appropriately named standard-bearer and
equally apt colours. "Fifty-four battering rams
and twelve slings . . . every one of pure gold"
(the Bible has sixty-six books) are taken as
equipment. Immanuel and Diabolus hold a
parley, but their differences are not accommo-
dated, so the city is besieged.

So the day being come, the command was
given, and the Prince's men stood bravely to
their arms; nor did, as before, bend their forces
against Ear-gate and Eye-gate. The word
[password] was then, Mansoul is won; so they
made their assault upon the town. Diabolus,
also, as fast as he could, with the main of his
power, made resistance from within, and his
high lords and chief captains for a time fought
very cruelly against the Prince's army.

But after three or four notable charges by the
Prince and his noble captains, Ear-gate was
broke open, and the bars and bolts wherewith
it was used to be fast shut up against the Prince,
were broken into a thousand pieces. Then did
the Prince's trumpets sound, the captains shout,
the town shake, and Diabolus retreat to his hold.
Well, when the Prince's forces had broke open
the gate, himself came up, and did set up his
throne in it. . . . Now from the Ear-gate the
street was strait, even to the house of him who

was the recorder before Diabolus took the town; and hard by his house stood the castle, which Diabolus for a long time had made his irksome den. The captains therefore quickly cleared the street by the use of their slings, so that way was made up to the heart of the town. Then the Prince commanded that Captain Boanerges, Captain Conviction, and Captain Judgment should forthwith march up the town to the old gentleman's gate. Then did the captains in most warlike manner enter into the town of Mansoul, and marching in with flying colours, they came up to the recorder's house (and that was almost as strong as the castle). Battering rams they took also with them, to plant against the castle gates. . . . Now the old gentleman, not knowing as yet fully their design, kept his gates shut all the time of this fight. Wherefore Boanerges demanded entrance at his gates; and no man making answer, he gave it one stroke with the head of a ram, and this made the old gentleman shake, and his house tremble and totter. Then came Mr. Recorder down to the gate, as well as he could, with quivering lips, he asked who was there.

Boanerges followed his answer with another stroke of the battering ram and the three captains gained admittance. "Now the recorder's house was a place of much convenience for Immanuel, not only because it was near and fronted the castle, the den where now Diabolus was. . . . As for Mr. Recorder, the captains carried it very reservedly to him: as yet he knew nothing of the great designs of Immanuel, so that he did not know what judgment to make, nor what would be the end of such thundering beginnings." The old gentleman and all who saw how "the captains carried it strangely to him" were "riveted in their fears" and he confessed that he had been at fault. "I have transgressed greatly, in keeping silence when I should have spoken; and in perverting justice when I should have executed the same. . . . O I tremble to think what will be the end of this so dreadful and so ireful a beginning."

Immanuel is victorious and Diabolus is called upon to surrender. "But, oh how loth was the beast to appear! How he stuck at it, how he shrunk! How he cringed!" He was bound in chains and publicly stripped of his armour. The inhabitants petition for pardon and at length receive it. Incredulity and others are brought to trial. (By contrast with Faithful at Vanity Fair, and with Bunyan himself before Sir John Kelynge, they are given every consideration and their legal rights are fully respected.) Imman-

148

uel remodels the town and a ministry is established, "for, said he, you of yourselves, unless you have teachers and guides, will not be able to know, and if not to know, to be sure not to do, the will of my Father."

There is an interesting detail here, reflecting Bunyan's view of the Christian ministry. Along with one teacher who was a native of Mansoul (and it is Mr. Conscience who is given this post), there is to be one from Shaddai's court.

He is a person of no less quality and dignity than my Father and I. And he is the lord chief secretary of my Father's house; for he is, and always has been, the chief dictator of all my Father's laws; a person well-skilled in all mysteries, and knowledge of mysteries, as is my Father, or as myself is. Indeed he is one with us in nature, and also as to loving of, and being faithful to, and in the eternal concerns of the town of Mansoul. . . . This teacher, therefore, must have the pre-eminence (both in your affections and judgment) before your other teacher; his personal dignity, the excellency of his teaching, also the great dexterity he hath to assist you to make and draw up petitions to my Father for your help and to his pleasing, must lay obligations upon you to love him, fear him, and to take heed that you grieve him not.

Mr. Conscience is warned that though he has been appointed preacher to the town he must himself be a scholar and learner and willing to go to the other teacher—whose identity, though he is never named, is obvious—for information "in all high and supernatural things." And he is enjoined to be content with his station. He may tell Mansoul anything he learns from "the lord chief secretary," but "he shall not attempt, or presume, to pretend to be a revealer of those high mysteries himself." Those who have followed, in our earlier chapters, the discussions of religious conditions in Bunyan's time will see at once the application of these words to the operations of the Holy Spirit and to the function of the Christian Ministry.

Here, one might suppose, Bunyan can close his story, but he seems unable to part with his characters. Or is it, perhaps, that he knows Mansoul is not yet safe? There are Diabolonians left in the town. Can they be trusted? His answer is given in the story of revolt organized by these doubtful characters, Mr. Mischief, Lord Lascivious, Lord Murder, Mr. Carnalsecurity, Mr. Profane, and their friends. They communicate with Diabolus and in his reply he urges them to "pry into, and endeavour to spy

out, the weakness of the town of Mansoul." He
asks them to send him word by what means he
may best "attempt the regaining thereof, to wit,
whether by persuasion to a vain and loose life,"
or "by tempting them to doubt and despair,"
or "by blowing up the town by the gunpowder
of pride and self-conceit." The plot is discovered and precautions are taken to withstand the
army of doubters which Diabolus is sending
against the town. Then the inhabitants ask the
"lord chief secretary" to send a petition on their
behalf asking Shaddai's aid. He is willing but
tells them they "must be present at the doing
of it." "True, the hand and pen shall be mine,
but the ink and paper must be yours, else how
can you say it is your petition?" To make a
similar point in *Pilgrim's Progress* Bunyan
would probably have introduced texts about the
intercession of the Holy Spirit on man's behalf,
but here he trusts his allegory to carry its meaning.

The stubbornness of the inhabitants leads
Lucifer to plan a fresh stratagem.

I have also another stratagem in my head. You
know Mansoul is a marked town, a town that
delights in commerce; what, therefore, if some

of our Diabolonians shall feign themselves far countrymen, and shall go out and bring to the market of Mansoul some of our wares to sell; and what matter at what rate they sell their wares, though it be but for half the worth? Now let those that thus trade in the market be those that are witty and true to us, and I will lay my crown to pawn, it will do. There are two that are come to my thoughts already, that I think will be arch at this work, and they are, Mr. Penny-wise-pound-foolish, and Mr. Get-i'th'-hundred-and-lose-i'th'-shire; nor is this man with the long name at all inferior to the other. What also if you join with them Mr. Sweet-world and Mr. Present-good, they are men that are civil and cunning, and our true friends and helpers. Let these, with as many more, engage in this business for us, and let Mansoul be taken up with much business, and let them grow fat and rich, and this is the way to get ground of them; remember ye not, that thus we prevailed upon Laodicea, and how many at present do we hold in this snare? Now when they begin to grow full they will forget their misery, and, if we shall not affright them, may happen to fall asleep, and so be got to neglect their town-watch, their castle-watch, as well as their watch at the gates.

Yea, may we not by this means so cumber Mansoul with abundance, that they shall be forced to make of their castle a warehouse, instead of a garrison fortified against us, and a receptacle of war? Thus if we get our goods and commodities thither, I reckon that the castle is more than half ours. Besides, could we so order it, that they should be filled with such kind of wares, then if we made a sudden assault upon them, it would be hard for the captain to take shelter there. Do you know that of the parable, "The deceitfulness of riches chokes the word"; and again, "When the heart is overcharged with surfeiting and drunkenness, and the cares of this life, all mischief comes upon them unawares."

Immanuel again saves the town in its extremity and enters amidst the joyful acclaim of its people. He addresses them at length and recites his hopes for them.

My Mansoul, I have oft-times delivered thee from the designs, plots, attempts, and conspiracies of Diabolus, and for all this I ask thee nothing, but that thou render not to me evil for my good, but that thou bear in mind my love and the continuance of my kindness to my beloved Mansoul, so as to provoke thee to walk, in thy measure, according to the benefits bestowed on thee. . . . Remember, therefore, O my Mansoul, that thou art beloved of me; as I have therefore taught thee to watch, to fight, to pray and to make war against my foes, so now I command thee to believe that my love is constant to thee. O my Mansoul, now have I set my heart, my love upon thee, watch: "behold I lay none other burden upon thee, than what thou hast already; hold fast till I come."

CHAPTER X

More of the Pilgrim Way

"What a universe of things is the heart of man!
. . . All the places and all the persons and all
the adventures that John Bunyan saw in his
sleep are all in your heart and in mine. All the
cities, all the roads that lead from one city to
another, with all the paths and all the by-paths
—all the adventures, experiences, endurances,
conflicts, overthrows, victories—all are within
us and never are to be seen anywhere else."—
Alexander Whyte.

SIX years after the publication of *Pilgrim's
Progress,* in 1684, there appeared a "Second
Part, wherein is set forth the manner of the setting out of Christian's wife and children, their
dangerous journey, and safe arrival at the
desired country." A prologue in verse gives
Bunyan an opportunity to reply to his critics and also to acknowledge the warm reception
the first part had generally received. He com-
plains that some have counterfeited his Pilgrim
and his name, and yet others "half my name and

title too have stitched to their book, to make them do." Addressing his new book he says,

If such thou meet'st with, then thine only way
Before them all, is, to say thy say
In thine own native language, which no man
Now useth, nor with ease dissemble can.

Criticism has apparently been levelled at the Pilgrim. Some say "he laughs too loud" (imagine *Pilgrim's Progress* offending by its undue gaiety!); others say "his head is in a cloud." Bunyan defends both his humour and the alleged obscurity of his allegorical method. There are things, he says, that a man on a pilgrimage sees which "make one's fancy checkle, while his heart doth ache." As for his obscurity,

I also know a dark similitude
Will on the fancy more itself intrude,
And will stick faster in the heart and head,
Than things from similes not borrowed.

Without undue modesty Bunyan recites the successes of Part I. Of his Pilgrim "thousands daily sing and talk."

In France and Flanders, where men kill each
        other,

My Pilgrim is esteem'd a friend, a brother.
In Holland too, 'tis said, as I am told,
My Pilgrim is with some worth more than gold.
Highlanders and wild Irish can agree
My Pilgrim should familiar with them be.
'Tis in New England under such advance,
Receives there so much loving countenance,
As to be trimm'd, new clothed, and decked with
    gems. . . .

Some who at first gave the Pilgrim a cold reception and "call'd him fool and noddy" now commend him "And to those whom they love, they do him send."

Part II is not quite as long as its predecessor, but to the reader it seems longer. Its art is more conscious. "I will make bold to talk metaphorically," is a telltale phrase once used. As one has put it, "the book swings to and fro between art and experience." There is as great skill—perhaps greater—in delineation of character, but the allegory breaks down at times. There is playfulness and a welcome humour, but it rather discredits the solemnity it relieves than serves the purpose of the story. This said, however, it remains true that the second part has been unduly overshadowed by the first. There is a breadth of sympathy and a warmth of human fellowship in the story of Christiana and her companions which we miss in Christian's story. Part II is the work of a mind more fully schooled in experience, less occupied with the tragic possibilities of life. It is from the pen not of a prisoner but of a busy and popular preacher; the preacher is naturally able to take a more cheerful view of life. The later party of pilgrims is a merry group, despite the occasional alarms and adventures. There are hospitable innkeepers, there is a marriage, and we discover that "Christiana, if need was [saving salt of Puritanism in that qualification!], could play upon the viol, and Mercy upon the lute"; so "since they were so merry disposed, she played them a lesson, and Ready-to-halt would dance. So he took Despondency's daughter, named Much-afraid, by the hand, and to dancing they went in the road. True, he could not dance without one crutch in his hand, but I promise you he footed it well: also the girl was to be commended, for she answered the music handsomely." This will be a new Bunyan to those who know him only through the Pilgrim who found that "the ease that pilgrims have is but little in this life."

Christiana felt the loss of her husband after

he had gone over the river and could be heard from no more. She wondered whether her unbecoming behaviour to her husband "was not one cause that she saw him no more," and this reflection "loaded her with guilt." "Yea, there was not anything that Christian either said to her, or did before her, all the while that his burden did hang upon his back, but it returned upon her like a flash of lightning, and rent the caul of her heart in sunder." In a dream she sees a parchment record of her sins and cries out for mercy. Two "very ill-favoured ones standing by her bedside" agree that they must "by one way or other seek to take her off from the thoughts of what shall be here after, else all the world cannot help it but she will become a pilgrim." A pilgrim she does become, in spite of Mrs. Timorous and other neighbours, and she sets out with her four boys and a young neighbour, Mercy.

Christiana, we may note in passing, is a forceful character, not disposed to take without question the arrangements made for pilgrims. She is not too conventional to have a kind thought even for Madam Wanton. She asks Great-heart for a sermon but she insists upon discussing its points.

The party "make a shift to get staggeringly over the Slough of Despond" and after much knocking are admitted through the Wicket-gate. The devil, in the shape of a barking cur, almost dissuades them from sufficient perseverance in their prayer. At the Interpreter's House they are heartily welcomed. When those that attended upon pilgrims came into the room "one smiled, and another smiled, and they all smiled for joy that Christiana was become a pilgrim." They were shown things that Christian did not see, including the man with the muck-rake.

The Interpreter has them first into a room where was a man that could look no way but downwards, with a muck-rake in his hand. There stood also one over his head with a celestial crown in his hand, and proffered to give him that crown for his muck-rake; but the man did neither look up nor regard, but raked to himself the straws, the small sticks, and dust of the floor.

Then said Christiana, I persuade myself that I know somewhat the meaning of this; for this is a figure of a man of this world; is it not, good sir?

Interpreter. Thou hast said the right, said he; and his muck-rake doth show his carnal mind. And whereas thou seest him rather give

heed to rake up straws and sticks and the dust
of the floor, than to do what he says that calls to
him from above with the celestial crown in his
hand, it is to show that heaven is but as a fable
to some, and that things here are counted the
only things substantial. Now whereas it was
also showed thee, that the man could look no
way but downwards, it is to let thee know that
earthly things, when they are with power upon
men's minds, quite carry their hearts away from
God.

Christiana. Then said Christiana, O deliver
me from this muck-rake!

From the house of the Interpreter the pilgrims are given a conductor, Mr. Great-heart,
who is well armed and brave. Like many a valiant soldier in the parliamentary army, and like
Captain Boanerges in *The Holy War,* he can
preach an effective sermon on occasion. "Truly,"
wrote Cromwell once, "I think that he that
prays and preaches best will fight best." He
can tell a camp-fire tale about a troublesome
recruit and his adventures—Mr. Fearing, who
"carried a Slough of Despond in his mind." He
can propound a riddle to mine host and be as
merry as any at the table. He dispatches giants
in desperate encounters, in which he shows himself as chivalrous as he is brave.

One of those who joins the party is old Mr. Honest. His portrait is cleverly drawn. He sums up the experience of practical idealists. "It happeneth to us as it happeneth to wayfaring men, sometimes our way is clean, sometimes foul, sometimes up-hill, sometimes down-hill, we are seldom at a certainty. The wind is not always at our backs, nor is every one a friend whom we meet within the way. We have met with some notable rubs already. . . . For the most part we find it true, that has been talked of, of old, A good man must suffer trouble." True, he came from Stupidity, four degrees further away from the sun than the City of Destruction. But he is on the way to the Celestial City and in time he reaches it. He plays a worthy part and helps Great-heart by slaying Diffidence, the wife of Giant Despair, with one blow. At the house of Gaius he can both put and answer riddles, but while the rest sit up all night engaged in pious discourse he makes no effort to conceal his drowsiness. At the river he has an easy crossing, because in his lifetime he "had spoken to one Good-conscience to meet him there," and he was helped over. His last words were, "Grace reigns."

A character who does not appear, but whose story is told by Great-heart, gives Bunyan scope for a display of great insight into a type we should not have expected him to describe sympathetically. This is Mr. Fearing, who "was always afraid that he should come short of whither he had a desire to go." Nothing shows better the mellowing of Bunyan's thought than the sentences in which he describes how this timid man, whose fear was for his salvation but who had the grace to venture on, was dealt with by the King of the country he sought. Fearing "lay roaring at the Slough of Despond for above a month together; nor durst he, for all he saw several go over before him, venture, though they, many of them, offered to lend him their hand. *He would not go back neither."* Even when, one sunshiny day, he at last ventured, he could hardly believe he was over.

At the House of the Interpreter he was still timid, and it was here that Great-heart first saw him.

He lay thereabout in the cold a good while, before he would adventure to call; Yet he would not go back. And the nights were long and cold then. Nay, he had a note of necessity in his bosom to my Master to receive him, and grant him the comfort of his house, and also to allow him a stout and valiant conductor because he was himself so chicken-hearted a man; and yet, for all that, he was afraid to call at the door. So he lay up and down thereabouts, till, poor man, he was almost starved. Yea, so great was his dejection, that though he saw several others for knocking got in, yet he was afraid to venture. At last, I think I looked out of the window, and perceiving a man to be up and down about the door, I went out to him, and asked what he was; but, poor man, the water stood in his eyes. So I perceived what he wanted. I went therefore in, and told it in the house, and we showed the thing to our Lord: so he sent me out again, to entreat him to come in; but I dare say I had hard work to do it. At last he came in, and I will say that for my Lord, he carried it wonderful lovingly to him. There were but a few good bits at the table, but some of it was laid upon his trencher. Then he presented the note, and my Lord looked thereon, and said his desire should be granted. So when he had been there a good while he seemed to get some heart, and to be a little more comfortable.

At the Valley of Humiliation, however, Fearing had no difficulty. "He cared not how mean he was, so he might be happy at last. . . . There was a kind of sympathy betwixt that valley and him." The Valley of the Shadow of Death did affright him, but it was quiet when he went through. "I suppose," says Great-heart, "those enemies had now a special check from our Lord, and a command not to meddle until Mr. Fearing was passed over it." And at the last river, when he was "in a heavy case" and sure he must be drowned, "the water was lower at this time than ever I saw it in all my life," and he went over "not much above wet-shod." Great-heart adds, "I never had a doubt about him; he was a man of a choice spirit, only he was always kept very low, and that made his life so burdensome to himself, and so troublesome to others."

In the Valley of Humiliation, where Christian had vanquished Apollyon, Christiana's party found no terrors. As Great-heart said, "Here is nothing to hurt us, unless we procure it to ourselves." They find it a meadow-land and they hear a shepherd boy singing, as he keeps his sheep, a song in praise of humility. The boy was "in very mean clothes, but of a very fresh and well-favoured countenance."

Hark, said Mr. Great-heart, to what the shepherd's boy saith: so they hearkened, and he said,

He that is down, needs fear no fall,
   He that is low, no pride;
He that is humble, ever shall
   Have God to be his guide.
I am content with what I have,
   Little be it, or much;
And, Lord, contentment still I crave,
   Because thou savest such.
Fulness to such a burden is
   That go on pilgrimage;
Here little, and hereafter bliss,
   Is best from age to age.

Then said their guide, Do you hear him? I will dare to say that this boy lives a merrier life, and wears more of that herb called heart's ease in his bosom, than he that is clad in silk and velvet.

At the close of the story, the crossing of the river by each member of the party is described. When Christiana goes over, "all the banks beyond the river were full of horses and chariots, which were come down from above to accompany her to the city gate. So she came forth and entered the river, with a beckon of farewell to those that followed her to the riverside. The last word she was heard to say here, was, I come, Lord, to be with thee, and bless thee."

Mr. Ready-to-halt bequeathed his crutches to his son "with a hundred warm wishes that he may prove better than I have done." His last words were, "Welcome life!"

Mr. Feeble-mind said, "As to my feeble mind, that I will leave behind me; for that I have no need of that in the place whither I go; nor is it worth bestowing upon the poorest pilgrim. . . . His last words were, Hold out, faith and patience."

Mr. Despondency's will was that his and his daughter's "desponds and slavish fears" should be by no man ever received. His last words were, "Farewell night; welcome day!" His daughter went singing through the river, "but none could understand what she said."

Mr. Valiant-for-truth made a will. "My sword I give to him that shall succeed me in my pilgrimage, and my courage and skill to him that can get it. My marks and scars I carry with me, to be a witness for me that I have fought His battles who now will be my rewarder." Many accompanied him to the riverside, "into which as he went he said, 'Death, where is thy sting?' And as he went down deeper, he said, 'Grave, where is thy victory?'

So he passed over, and all the trumpets sounded for him on the other side."

The Dreamer's vision did not last till Christiana's four boys, with their wives and children, had passed over. Indeed, since he had returned from that country the Dreamer heard that they were still alive "and so would be for the increase of the Church in that place where they were for a time."

CHAPTER XI

Bunyan's Literary Indebtedness

THAT a tinker of Elstow should have written books known throughout the world, and in one case translated into more than a hundred languages and dialects, is startling enough to justify the question whether he had access to and used literary models. That there are literary parallels to his *Pilgrim's Progress,* both in its general conception and in some details, is easily established. How far they supplied Bunyan with either ideas or inspiration, it is less easy to say. He himself claimed the spontaneity we associate with the work of genius. He was busy, he tells us, on another book, when, almost before he was aware, he found himself beginning his allegory.

And thus it was: I, writing of the way
And race of saints, in this our gospel day,
Fell suddenly into an allegory
About their journey, and the way to glory,
In more than twenty things which I set down;

This done, I twenty more had in my crown,
And they again began to multiply,
Like sparks that from the coals of fire do fly.

Even yet he did not think to show the world
what he had written "in such a mode,"

        . . . nor did I undertake
Thereby to please my neighbour: no, not I;
I did it mine own self to gratify.

In vacant seasons—in prison, we must remember—he thus diverted his thoughts from less
worthy things. As he wrote, the theme grew.
"Still as I pull'd, it came." He asked advice of
his friends,

And some said, Let them live; some, Let them
       die;
Some said, John, print it; others said, Not so;
Some said, It might do good; others said, No.

Evidently allegory was not wholly congenial to
some of the stricter sort, so Bunyan defended his
method.

      . . . fish there be, that neither hook, nor line,
Nor snare, nor net, nor engine can make thine;
They must be grop'd for, and be tickled too,
Or they will not be catch'd, whate'er you do.

So, apparently, Bunyan hopes to reach by his allegory those who will not hear or heed his sermons. Even as "a pearl may be found in a toad's head" (readers of Shakespeare will recognize the phrase, but it was probably proverbial and its use is no argument for borrowing), so his book may contain some things that excel. Criticized because allegory "wants solidness," he points to the "types, shadows, and metaphors" in which, in olden time, the gospel was set forth.

"Bunyan drew more from the world around him than from books." Before he wrote the song, "Who would true valour see," he may have heard Shakespeare's "Who doth ambition shun" (*As You Like It,* Act II, scene v), but the indebtedness was limited to a word here and there. He may have heard lines from Spenser's *Faërie Queene* describing the Celestial City or the giant who must be slain by the hero, or Milton's lines from *Il Penseroso* on "forests and enchantments drear," but more probably an explanation of the similarities which have suggested such dependence is simply that all drew upon conventional imagery.

In his *Sighs from Hell* (an elaboration of the parable of Dives and Lazarus) Bunyan makes the rich man say, referring to his life on earth, "The Scriptures, thought I then, what are they? A dead letter, a little ink and paper, of three or four shillings price. Alack! What is Scripture? Give me a ballad, a newsbook, George on Horseback, or Bevis of Southampton. Give me some book that teaches curious Arts, that tells old Fables." It is not far-fetched to suggest that Bunyan refers here to chap-books and other popular literature with which he was acquainted in his youth, and we need not be surprised to find that *Pilgrim's Progress* here and there recalls Sir Bevis of Southampton. The fight with Apollyon is particularly suggestive in parallels. From such ballads and romances, then, which were popular amongst humble folk long after cavalier society had become too sophisticated to enjoy them, Bunyan may have derived some details in the adventures of his pilgrims, such as the Enchanted Land, the dragons, and the giants. To *Emblems, Divine and Moral,* by Francis Quarles, which was popular with Puritans, he may have owed suggestions for some of his allegorical details, especially in describing the Interpreter's House. Certainly it is to Baily's *Practice of Piety,* one of the two books his wife brought him,

wherein, as he tells us, he "found some things
that were somewhat pleasing," that we may trace
the idea of the theological discussions that have
discouraged some readers of the *Pilgrim's
Progress*. But a glance at this book, so popular
in Bunyan's day, at once reveals his superiority.
His restraint is remarkable compared with
Baily's "fearless and heavy tread through so
many limited and impossible doctrines." He
does not hesitate to say, in a marginal note, "the
Latin I borrow," when he puts into the mouth of
Dr. Skill a prescription for Matthew's trouble.

The literary history of the main conception of
the pilgrimage is interesting and carries us back
as far at least as the *Pilgrimage of the Sowle,*
printed by Caxton in 1483, a translation of a
book by a monk of Chaliz, Guillaume de Guileville, written in 1330, who in turn acknowledged
his dependence on the *Romance of the Rose*
(1230). Here is a dream, a sight of the city
of heaven in a mirror, and a description of the
people who live there. The pilgrim meets
Grace-Dieu, who keeps the wicket-gate. He
must pass through the waters of baptism before
he may come to her house. He is there attended
by personifications of the virtues, shown rarities,
and provided with the scrip of Faith, a staff

called Hope, and some heavy armour. The last
he declines, preferring like David to take his
familiar equipment. He has adventures and is
attacked by Avarice, Heresy, Idolatry, and
others. He makes his prayer to the Virgin.
After purification in a sacred fountain, he is
offered a choice of monasteries for refuge and
is welcomed to Cisteaux Abby. Death runs him
through the body with his scythe and the
Dreamer awakes with a start. He is brought
back to earth by the sound of convent bells and
cock-crowing, and commends his story to those
who are good winnowers and able to select truth
from falsehood, just as Bunyan in his "Conclusion" tells his reader to throw away the dross
and keep the gold.

Many subsequent allegories reproduce either
the device of the dream or the pilgrimage motif.
Three of these appeared shortly before or during Bunyan's lifetime. But the pilgrimages narrated are generally ordinary journeys to popular
shrines and the books contain meditations rather
than allegories. Patrick's *Parable of the Pilgrim,* published in 1665, while Bunyan was in
prison and only a few years before he wrote
Pilgrim's Progress, uses a pilgrimage as a parable of the godly life. Otherwise it has little in

174

common with *Pilgrim's Progress*. It was designed particularly to demonstrate the superiority of the Established Church over the dissenting communions. The reader is halfway through the book before the pilgrim sets out. There is a reminder of Bunyan's Delectable Mountains in Patrick's hill-top from which a group of people are found by his pilgrims viewing the heavenly Jerusalem. The idea of life as a pilgrimage also appears in George Herbert's *Temple* and in the *Emblems* of Francis Quarles, both of which had a wide circulation in Bunyan's day.

How far Bunyan was unconsciously influenced by what was evidently a not uncommon figure of speech we can never know. Actual borrowing cannot be proved and was vigorously repudiated by Bunyan himself.

Some say the *Pilgrim's Progress* is not mine,
Insinuating as if I would shine
In name, and fame, by the work of another.

He tells us "John such dirt-heap never was since God converted him," and proceeds,

Manner and matter too, was all mine own,
Nor was it unto any mortal known

Till I had done it. Nor did any then
By books, by wits, by tongue, or hand, or pen,
Add five words to it, or wrote half a line
Thereof: the whole and ev'ry whit is mine.

One source upon which Bunyan obviously
drew we have not yet considered. We need not
seek in the by-ways of literature for the suggestion of the Valley of Shadow of Death; the
Twenty-third Psalm is at hand. The arming
of the Christian is told once for all when Paul
writes his letter to the Ephesians; de Guileville
has a wicket-gate, but the Gospels long before
told of a strait gate and contrasted it with the
wide gate that leads to destruction; the writer of
the Epistle to the Hebrews referred to many
who, like Abraham, had gone out to a place they
were to receive for an inheritance, not knowing
whither they went but travelling by faith as they
looked for the city, and he had called them pilgrims seeking a better country. The thought
of Christ as the Way and of the highway of
God in the desert pictured by Isaiah may also be
cited.

Bunyan's love for the Bible is made clear in
Grace Abounding. "The Bible was precious to
me in those days. And now methought I began
to look into the Bible with new eyes, and read as

I never read before. . . . And, indeed, then I
was never out of the Bible." It is emphasized
on every page in *Pilgrim's Progress,* which is
the story of a Man with a Book. At the Palace
Beautiful the pilgrim is shown "the records of
greatest antiquity" containing "the pedigree of
the Lord" and the worthy acts his servants had
done. Mercy asks the Shepherds to sell the
wonderful mirror, a "glass that was one of a
thousand." "It would present a man one way,
with his own features exactly, and, turn it but
another way, and it would show one the very
face and similitude of the Prince of pilgrims
himself." Mr. Valiant-for-truth carries a Sword
which is God's Word, and Mr. Ready-to-halt
leans on crutches which are the promises of the
Bible. Great-heart, at the Enchanted Ground,
led the party through "a place at which a man
is apt to lose his way." In the dark he "was put
to a stand; but he had in his pocket a map of all
ways leading to or from the Celestial City. . . .
Then thought I with myself, Who that goeth
on pilgrimage but would have one of those maps
about him?" A marginal note adds, "God's
Book."

It must be admitted that the attempt to press
the metaphors of the Bible into the service of

his allegory is often carried to extremes by Bunyan, as when Christian and Hopeful fall into the net of the Flatterer, presumably because the author recalled the text in Proverbs, "The flatterer spreadeth a net." The mistake is sometimes made, as it has been put, of "forcing Scripture and life alike into unreality." The allegorizing habit appears at such times as an obsession.

The simplicity and directness of his style and the quickening of his imagination Bunyan certainly owed in very large measure to his knowledge of the Bible. In prison, he tells us, he had his greatest "inlet into the word of God." "I have seen that here, which I am persuaded I shall never, in this world, be able to express." The extraordinary phenomenon the Bible presents—Oriental imagery under the control of strong, Hebraic moral purposes—perpetuates its influence over men's minds by at once stimulating the imagination and subordinating the flights of fancy to practical ends, by providing responsive minds with imagery for the expression of the transcendent and, at the same time, revealing human life in all its concrete details as evidence of an immanent spiritual meaning.

CHAPTER XII

How Bunyan Used His Freedom

KING CHARLES admitted in his Declaration
of Indulgence of 1672 that it was "evident
by the sad experience of twelve yeares" that there
was "very little fruit of all these forceable
courses," and Bunyan, as we saw, was one of
those who were released from prison. How he
used his freedom has already been partially
told. Between his release and his death in 1688
(leaving out the masterpiece written during
the brief imprisonment of 1675-76) he published twenty-seven works, and sixteen others
were left in manuscript, according to Charles
Doe's list, which is dated 1698. Of course, some
of these were only brief treatises expanding discourses he had delivered, but with *Mr. Badman, The Holy War,* and the second part of the
Pilgrim's Progress among them, they represent
substantial literary labours.

His primary occupation, however, was that
of preaching and exercising a widely-acknowl-

edged leadership among nonconformists, not only in and around Bedford but as far away as London, which he frequently visited. He was much in demand as a preacher, for he spoke only of what he "smartingly did feel," as he says. His popularity pleased him but he knew the danger that pride might easily be "blown up at the applause of every unadvised Christian." When he was complimented once and told that he had preached a "sweet sermon," he replied with bluntness, but for the good of his own as well as of his admirer's soul, "You need not remind me of that, the Devil told me of it before I was out of the pulpit."

In 1676 a religious census, ordered by the Archbishop and taken parish by parish—which still exists in manuscript—showed that there were three to four thousand nonconformists in Bedfordshire. Persecution had borne a fruit not looked for by the king's advisers.[1] There were stirring times in England in these years. The "Popish Plot" of 1679 created great excitement, but except for veiled allusions in *The Holy War* and in *Pilgrim's Progress, Part II*, Bunyan's works do not reflect the political situation. He was much occupied in the over-

---

[1] See page 32.

sight of his congregation and his task was sometimes the distressing one of discipline. Some
of the records of the Bedford Meeting are in
his own writing. Brother Oliver Thodye acknowledged in meeting "summe miscarages the
Church had charged him with as, namely,
breaking the Saboth and brawling with neighbours." One John Wildman was resentful of
Bunyan's discipline. He drew in writing a
charge against the congregation. In this he was
"found extriordinary guilty of a kind of railery
and very great passion very much condemned by
the whole congregation." He was judged guilty
of slander against "our beloved and honnered
brother Bunyan," for he had charged the pastor with prevailing upon women members to
reveal to him their husbands' financial resources
so that he might "put a levy opon them." Communion was withdrawn from him and expulsion
was threatened should he not repent. That was
in 1680. Three years later Wildman was again
a thorn in Bunyan's side, having sent a "frothy
letter" to the congregation. The reply, signed
by Bunyan and others, called on him not only
for repentance but for guarantees from those in
the country before whom he had accused Bunyan that he had shown the fruits of reformation.

Was Wildman one of the originals who contributed to Bunyan's composite picture of Mr. Badman?

Opposition to Bunyan was not particular as to its weapons. We cannot entirely overlook, in any story of his life, the charge which concerned his relations with Agnes Beaumont in 1674. Her father, who had lost interest in the nonconformist cause, discouraged her from attendance at the meetings. She had joined the Bedford Meeting, the first to be enrolled during the pastorate of Bunyan, who entered her name as Agniss Behemont. One day she went to her brother's house in order to accompany him to Gamlingay, where a meeting was to be held. She found that her brother could spare only the one horse that was to carry both him and his wife. Bunyan chanced to ride up on his way to the meeting and was asked to take Agnes with him, but he hesitated, saying, "Your father will be grievous angry if I do." The father saw them together and on her return locked the door against her, refusing her entrance till she should promise to break with the people of the Meeting. She was forced to spend the night in the barn and went in the morning to her brother's. Not for several days did she yield and return home. Two days afterwards her father died suddenly, the result of a strange seizure. A clergyman had seen Bunyan and Agnes riding together "at Gamlingay town-end" and spread the story. A lawyer whose suit Agnes had but lately rejected charged her with poisoning her father, and Bunyan with complicity. The funeral was deferred and an inquest held. This completely exonerated the two and brought shame on their enemies. The story was afterwards committed to writing by Agnes, who lived nearly fifty years longer, for the sake of Bunyan's reputation. In one of the later editions of *Grace Abounding,* in no uncertain terms but without specific reference to this incident, he repudiates the implied charges. We need not reproduce more than two or three sentences from his statement. "My foes have missed their mark in thus shooting at me. I am not the man. . . . I find these lies and slanders to me as ornament. It belongs to my Christian profession to be vilified, slandered, reproached, and reviled; and since all this is nothing else, as my God and my conscience do bear me witness, I rejoice in reproaches for Christ's sake."

It would please some, no doubt, to find new ground for the revival of such charges against the author of *Pilgrim's Progress,* if that were possible. But as yet the complete vindication, after investigation, given him by a community in which he had as many enemies as friends, stands out to support the emphatic statements he published in the last year of his life.

The two or three years preceding the Revolution of 1688 saw a renewal of persecution. The ill-starred Monmouth rebellion was followed by the bloody reign of terror which made the name of Lord Jeffreys a byword to nonconformists. The aged Richard Baxter and many others were imprisoned at the instance of busy informers and officious ecclesiastical courts. Separatists had to worship in secluded places and often by night with sentinels on guard. Persecution became systematic and thorough. Bunyan realized his danger and made his will, "divers good causes and considerations" moving him "at this present especially." It shows us that his second wife, Elizabeth, who had made so brave an appeal for justice on his behalf, was still his beloved companion. It also shows us that he was in reasonably comfortable circumstances and contrasts in that particular with the will of his father, who died in 1676 and

184

left John one shilling! He describes himself simply as "John Bunyan, brazier." Probably he laboured at times with his hands while a minister; at any rate, we see that to the end he avoided all emphasis upon the separation of the clergy from other men which is involved in ecclesiastical views of the ministry. He was simply one member of the church appointed to carry out certain responsibilities on its behalf, and to this day this is the characteristic nonconformist attitude to ordination. The will did not come to light till the nineteenth century, when it was found hidden away in a recess in Bunyan's Bedford house.

By 1687 James II was cultivating the good will of nonconformists for reasons of his own, and Bunyan, now influential among them, was actually approached, according to one of his friends, with an offer of some position of trust in the king's gift. But Bunyan had seen the consequences, for local government, of royal reorganization of the ancient corporations, and he "laboured with his congregation to prevent their being imposed on in this kind. . . . When a great man, coming to Bedford on some such errand, sent for him, as it is supposed to give him a place of public trust, he would by no means come at him, but sent his excuse."

The same friend says that Bunyan often went to London when at leisure from writing and preaching and was much liked by congregations of nonconformists there. Among his London friends was the eminent divine, Dr. John Owen, who once told King Charles that he would gladly exchange his learning for the tinker's power as a preacher. Pinner's Hall, Girdler's Hall, Salter's Hall, and other guild halls were used before there were nonconformist church buildings, and in at least one of these Bunyan preached. In London the nonconformists were not all people of humble birth and condition. Such well-known people as General Charles Fleetwood, Cromwell's son-in-law, Sir John Hartop, Sir Thomas Overbury, and the Countess of Anglesey were all in Owen's congregation, which Bunyan sometimes addressed. He knew well one Lord Mayor of London, Sir John Shorter. One of the city merchants offered to take his son Joseph into business without the usual premium, but Bunyan, independent to the end, replied that God had sent him not to advance his family but to preach the gospel.

Charles Doe, a comb-maker, who had a shop near London Bridge, heard Bunyan preach at a private house "So New Testament-like that he made me admire, and weep for joy, and give him my affections." He secured an introduction by letter and remained a devoted admirer. To him we owe the preservation of information about Bunyan's life to supplement his own meagre autobiographical statements. Doe tells us Bunyan was very popular. "If there were but one day's notice given, there would be more people come together to hear him preach than the meeting-house could hold." Doe saw as many as twelve hundred gather at seven o'clock on a working-day morning—and that "in the dark winter time." But Bunyan refused to leave the country for a city charge and remained loyal to his worthy Bedford friends.

One August day in 1688 Bunyan set out for London, but he had been asked to lend his aid in reconciling a father and his son so he turned his horse towards Reading. There he "used such pressing arguments" with the father "against anger and passion" that the old man was pacified. He rode from Reading to London in drenching rain and stayed with a good

187

friend, John Strudwick. On the 19th of the month he preached at Whitechapel; it was his last sermon. He was in a worn-out condition, and the exposure of his journey had been too great for his weakened constitution. He fell dangerously ill but bore his sufferings with exemplary patience until he passed away on the last day of the month. His passing was like that of Valiant-for-truth and for him too "all the trumpets sounded on the other side."

A pilgrimage to Bunyan's tomb takes one to one of London's interesting burial grounds. By the busy thoroughfare of City Road, originally the Old Royal Road, one reaches on one side of the street the Wesleyan Chapel in which John and Charles Wesley so long ministered, and exactly opposite is the old Dissenter's Burying Ground of Bunhill Fields. The earliest map, and still earlier traditions, attribute to this spot the position of a tumulus which gave to two fields the name of Bone-hill fields, and this burying ground of great antiquity became what Southey has called the *Campo Santo* of the nonconformists. If those old moss-covered stones could speak, what tales they could tell of suffering for righteousness' sake, of valiant battles to gain the vantage ground on which we of to-

day stand. Here are the graves of many who
died martyrs for their faith, living in the gloomy
dungeons of Newgate and Fleet prisons until
death released them from the cruelties of men.
Here one finds the graves of such stalwarts as
John Owen, Thomas Goodwin and Thankful
Owen, Nathaniel Mather, from whom Increase
Mather was descended, Thomas Bradbury, Su-
sannah Wesley, Theophilus Lindsey and, of
later date, Isaac Watts, William Blake, and
Daniel Defoe.

Unlike many of the tombs, that of John Bunyan is in good preservation and bears on it this
inscription, "John Bunyan, Author of 'Pilgrim's
Progress.' Ob. 31st. August, 1688, Aet. 60. Restored by public subscription under the presi-
dency of the Rt. Hon. the Earl of Shaftesbury,
May, 1862." In this tomb are buried also John
Strudwick, in whose house Bunyan died, and
several others.

The Burying Ground is now open to the public and the open spaces with seats are a boon to
the dwellers in the congested, poverty-stricken
districts near-by. Perhaps some of the peace
and fortitude of the men who have here found
their final resting place may enter the souls of
the jaded, weary human beings who frequent the

burying ground; perhaps to the passers-by may come feelings of reverence for those sainted ones —confessors, historians, pastors, poets—who having fought the good fight, here rest in God's Acre, the very dust of which is sacred.

CHAPTER XIII

Bunyan's Genius

"In niches and on pedestals around about the hall stood statues and busts. . . . Shakespeare, Spenser, Milton, and Bunyan, moulded of homeliest clay but instinct with celestial fire."—*Hawthorne, "The Hall of Fantasy."*

OUR discussion of Bunyan's dependence upon literary sources left us very sure that he was no imitator or plagiarist. His reading of the Bible was his chief, if not his only, schooling in style. His materials he drew from the life about him; the strong cross-currents of inclination and conscience gave him for dramatic treatment situations of universal interest. His genius lay in the completeness with which he gave expression to that exalted mood of the human spirit which, in Puritanism, touched common things and common people with greatness; but his genius is not less seen in the freedom and creative independence which enabled him to temper, chasten, and direct that mood.

191

Puritans rejected romances in the interest of a strict ideal of truth. But, receiving the Bible and all its contents as an unquestionably true record of God's dealings with man, they unwittingly accepted a great body of literature in which romance, while it is subordinated to moral purpose, gives great human interest to the doings of men and women in a distant age and a far different civilization. For the tinker of Elstow, walking along country lanes on a misty November morning or in the keen March wind, it must have been an experience of release to journey in imagination to the land of Beulah, with its sunny vineyards, its singing birds, and its happy bridal feasts amidst abundance of corn and wine. "Men who had cast themselves finally off from that gay and bright world in which English literature had dwelt for centuries, rekindled the extinguished light at the more ancient flame, and borrowed the colours of the more ancient poetry for their desolated world." (Kelman)

Yet the imagination which was quick to follow the imagery of other and distant ages and peoples played easily upon its immediate surroundings. Bunyan's writings are so full of "local color" as to be a valuable source for the student of his period. The fisherman, with his snares, hooks, and nets, and the fowler with his lime-twig, light, and bell; the smith's dog lying at the foot of the anvil, "although the fire-sparks flee in his face"; the chick that "every time she drank lift up her head and her eyes towards heaven"; the ancient cross on the village green and the bell-tower near-by; the mansion on Ampthill Heights, with its armory and collection of "rarities", its beautiful grounds and pleasant arbours; Sturbridge Fair, with its wares from many lands, its delights and games, its knaves and fools, and its court of justice; the high roads and byways of Bedfordshire and all the dangers and chances of travel in an age that feared its Claude Duvals, John Nevisons, and other highwaymen; even the fruit hanging over an orchard wall to tempt the youthful passer-by; the welcome inns and their jolly hosts; the weary travellers sleeping by the roadside or "leaning upon their staves to talk with any by the way"; the criminal hanging in irons for all to see—a thousand sights familiar to the observant man are all turned to good account with an artistry that is seldom conscious art.

We have already made the acquaintance of many of the men and women whom Bunyan watched with so much understanding of character and, as he grew older, with increasing sympathy and charity. There is appropriateness in all their names and often great skill in the way they are introduced to us. There is a Roundhead humour very different in its subtlety from the Cavalier wit we associate with Bunyan's times. We smile when, as Christian is trying this way and that to get out of the Slough of Despond, Help comes along and asks him what he does there. It is part of the helpfulness of Help that he can expose the ludicrous nature of many of our struggles with despondency. Christian delivers a wordy lecture to Hopeful about the right and wrong kinds of fear. Hopeful's reply is that of many a reader. "Well said; I believe you have said the truth. Are we now almost got past the Enchanted Ground?" A change of subject often helps! The courtship of Mercy by Mr. Brisk is a masterpiece of humour, gentle satire, and character analysis—a proof, Dr. Whyte calls it, of Bunyan's "health, strength, and truth to nature." We feel sure the eyes of the brave Puritan author twinkled as he told how "Mercy, looking behind her, saw, as she thought, something most like a lion, and it came a great padding pace after her."

If Bunyan can occasionally enliven edification with humour, he is also able to deal effectively with the macabre and the ghastly. The Valley of the Shadow of Death in Part II is described with a restraint that greatly enhances Bunyan's purpose. It is a place of evils that are felt but not seen by the pilgrims. They heard "a groaning, as of dead men. . . . Words of lamentations, as of some in extreme torment. . . . They thought that they felt the ground begin to shake under them, as if some hollow place was there; they heard also a kind of hissing as of serpents, *but nothing as yet appeared."* About the middle of the valley "Christiana said, Methinks I see something yonder upon the road before us, a thing of such a shape such as I have not seen. Then said Joseph, Mother, what is it? An ugly thing, child, an ugly thing, said she. But Mother, what is it like? 'Tis like I cannot tell what, says she. And now it was but a little way off. Then said she, it is nigh. Well, well, said Mr. Great-heart, let them that are most afraid keep close to me. So the fiend came on, and the conductor met it; but when it was just come to him, it vanished to all their sights."

There are absurdities, as in the scene of Matthew's cure and the questions the boy puts to Prudence, or in the golden anchor given to Christiana at the Palace Beautiful in case she should meet (on the highway!) turbulent weather. Sometimes the allegory gives way awkwardly to preaching. But the remarkable thing is that these defects are so few as to stand out in vivid contrast with Bunyan's usually skilful, subtle, and extraordinarily suggestive use of a difficult device.

Bunyan's success exposed him to the compliment of imitation. Among other works which were either put forth to capitalize his name and fame with deliberate piratical intent, or offered to the world as inspired supplements to his work, there appeared a Third Part of the *Pilgrim's Progress,* which, had it been his, might have fulfilled the hint contained in the last sentence of the genuine Second Part. "Shall it be my lot to go that way again," Bunyan had written, "I may give those that desire it an account of what I am here silent about." This book by "J.S." did not claim, as did a later Part III, to be Bunyan's work; the author wished to help promote the practice of giving pious books at funerals "instead of rings, gloves, wine, or bisket"! He hoped to prevent the "lightness and laughter" which the reading of some passages (in *Pilgrim's Progress*) "occasions in some light and frothy minds." A more mercenary motive seems to have inspired most of the numerous imitations of Bunyan which appeared during his life or shortly after his death, some of which went so far as to claim his name or initials for their title page.

CHAPTER XIV

What Bunyan Gave to Christian Faith and Order

The soul of religion is the practick part.
—Christian in "Pilgrim's Progress."

BUNYAN'S contribution to the religious life of his own and succeeding ages has been, and always will be, variously estimated. There have been Roman Catholic editions of *Pilgrim's Progress;* only a few omissions were needed to put a book loved by the most protesting of Protestants at the service of Catholic piety. Some readers find most readily in Bunyan a practical emphasis and a disparagement of both speculation and formalism; others see Bunyan's greatest insight in his sense of an omnipresent Providence and in his conviction that the soul has an inescapable responsibility; others, again, commend especially his understanding of the dangers which confront the Church and its ministry; least appreciated, perhaps, by those who have interpreted Bunyan to our later days is his broad sympathy and his recognition, in later life at least, of the variety of types of Christian character.

First place must be given to his exaltation of "the practick part" of religion. Bunyan is sternly critical of the religious profession which is content with talk. Talkative's house is "as empty of religion as the white of an egg is of savour." . . . The brute in his kind serves God far better than he. He is the very stain, reproach, and shame of religion to all that know him; it can hardly have a good word in all that end of the town where he dwells, through him. . . . A saint abroad, and a devil at home. . . . Men that have any dealings with him say it is better to deal with a Turk than with him. At the day of judgment "it will not be said, Did you believe? but, were you doers, or talkers only?" Talkative claims that "great knowledge of gospel mysteries" is a sign of the work of grace in the heart, to which Christian replies that such knowledge is no proof of a regenerate condition. "When Christ said, Do you know these things? and the disciples had answered, Yes; he addeth, Blessed are ye if ye do them. . . . A man may know like an angel, and yet be no Christian." Knowledge "that resteth in the bare speculation of things," is to be distinguished from that which is accompanied by faith and love, "which puts a man upon doing even the will of God from the heart."

The Pilgrim's earnest journeying to a better country and a city not built with hands is quite commonly taken to reveal in the author an other-worldliness quite sufficient to discredit him in an age which is well content with the world it is so busy enjoying. But the charge of otherworld-liness does great injustice to Bunyan. True, the ultimate sanctions and rewards of righteousness in which he put his faith could not be seen close at hand; they would not be fully known in the earthly pilgrimage. But the certainty that they existed only served to give a significance to the everyday life of men, a dignity to simple and humble virtues, and a dangerous power to sins both small and great. George Bernard Shaw was, of course, trying to shock a generation brought up on *Pilgrim's Progress* when he said, "The whole allegory is a consistent attack on morality and respectability, without a word that one can remember against vice and crime," but he showed great insight into Bunyan's ruling conviction. "This is the true joy of life, the being used for a purpose recognised by yourself as a mighty one; the being thoroughly worn out before you are thrown on the scrap heap; the being a force of nature instead of a feverish selfish clod of ailments and grievances complaining that the world will not devote itself to making you happy." (Epistle Dedicatory to *Man and Superman.*)

Such convictions at once demand and sustain a strenuous life in which constant effort alone guarantees success. "Man's spiritual existence," as Froude says, "is like the flight of a bird in the air. . . . When he ceases to exert himself he falls." Bunyan lived in days that tempted many to ease and indulgence, with their consequent undermining of the native vigour. They were days that needed the tonic of a sense of responsibility—and the need did not end with the seventeenth century. "When will men learn," asked Dr. Crothers, "that morality is not a town, but a road, and the truly moral thing is to keep moving?" There were many in Bedford, as in London, who were satisfied with an outward and a formal compliance with standards which were themselves unchanging, and it was such satisfaction, rather than Puritan earnestness, that made men's lives mean and narrow and bigoted. Bunyan, in the goodly fellowship of the prophets, preached in his books, as by word and example, a religion which will always find its apostles "so long as man believes that he has a soul and is responsible for his actions." This was a religion which laid upon a few, and Bunyan among them, the obligation to deal plainly with their neighbours. "There is but little of this faithful dealing with men nowadays," says Christian to Faithful. The records of the Bedford Meeting and the dislike of Puritans and Separatists among the complacent Cavaliers alike suggest that if there was little of such "faithful dealing" there were many for whom that little was too much!

Along with the presentation of his challenge to the consciences of men in a vernacular and with imagery easily understood by the unlettered, Bunyan offered his readers a keen analysis of the vicissitudes of the spiritual life. In this they saw themselves, their failures and their victories, in a new light. His insight was remarkable, but it appears, of course, far better in the continuous reading of his writings than in the citation of isolated examples. We will nevertheless select a few illustrations.

Pliable is a neighbour who urges Christian not to undertake the pilgrimage, but when Christian enumerates the things he is going out to see, and expects to find, Pliable finds his heart inclines to go with Christian. "I begin to come to a point; I intend to go along with this good man." That is a different kind of decision from Christian's and it is small wonder that Pliable was soon offended by the discomforts of the Slough of Despond and "got out of the mire on that side of the Slough which was next to his own house."

The wicket-gate is placed early in the Pilgrim's journey, and only those who go through it can hope to reach the City. But such early decision does not mean final freedom from choice; the Pilgrim has many adventures yet before him. In a sermon which Bunyan was seeing through the press a few days before he died he said, "Conversion is not the smooth, easy-going process some men seem to think it." It was this that, in a more memorable way, he had said in the story of his Pilgrim.

He saw how deceptive memory may be when we are recalling our earlier moods. At the Palace Beautiful, Christian says that he would gladly have stayed at the House of the Interpreter a twelvemonth, but if we turn back the pages we find that he was hurrying to move on even while the Interpreter was giving him illumination that was for his good. How often we think that we made the most of an experience long since ended when, as a matter of fact, we were actually so restless that we hurried on before it taught us all we might have learned!

Faithful and Hopeful are carefully assigned to accompany Christian during different parts of his journey. The genial mood of hope in later life will be safer, thought the Puritan, if it has been preceded by the more austere mood of discipline. These two characters symbolize moods of the human spirit that we call by names Bunyan never heard, but he understood them none the less. Hebraism and Hellenism are united in the complete experience of the Christian pilgrimage, as they are in the history of the Christian Church.

By-path Meadow is not reached from the highway without crossing a stile. Scruples must be overcome before we take the easy way. As has been said, "no man who is quarrelling with the road will travel long before he finds himself at a stile." On the meadow path Christian follows Vain Confidence walking ahead in the twilight; soon only his footsteps can be heard when darkness falls. Vain Confidence is Christian himself "mistaking his own will for wisdom" and impatient of the advice of Hopeful.

In the story of Little-faith we read that his adventure with the highwaymen cost him his pocket-money, but his jewels he fortunately saved; the place where these were "they never ransacked." Faint-heart, Mistrust, and Guilt had robbed the poor fellow of his spending money, so that he was thereafter "forced to beg as he went, to keep himself alive, for his jewels he might not sell." He had to lean on others, but his soul was still his own.

Atheist is introduced to us at a significant point. It is on the borders of Beulah, when the pilgrims are not far from the desired land, that he "falls into a very great laughter" at their credulity. "A less courageous writer," Dr. Whyte says, "a writer less sure of his ground, would have left out Atheist altogether . . . or introduced him at any other period" in the pilgrimage. But Bunyan knew how near to the highway lay great perils, how near indeed to the gates of the City lay a "by-path to hell." He had shown Christian being given "a pull" as he entered the wicket-gate, lest he fall a victim to the arrows of one who made it a practice to shoot pilgrims just as they arrived at their place of decision; he had shown us a Valley of Humiliation to be traversed and a monster to be slain immediately after the Pilgrim left the Palace Beautiful and its happy fellowship; from the Delectable Mountains he had shown us a view of the Celestial City, but one of these was "very steep on the further side," and at the bottom Christian could see "several men dashed all to pieces by a fall that they had from the top." Bunyan knew, in other words, that pride and self-satisfaction, or even sheer weariness and the reaction that follows every exalted mood, constituted as great a danger as the temptations to the grosser sins. There is point, then, in Atheist's challenge to the pilgrims when they are so near their goal.

How often Bunyan is misjudged by his one greatest book! It is supposed that he portrayed Christian as the one commendable type of pilgrim. As a matter of fact, he showed a many-sided sympathy and appreciation of a great variety of types of spiritual experience. He himself could not say at just what time he had become a Christian, and he refused to prescribe a Procrustes bed for the conscience of any other man. In the second part of the story of the

pilgrim, Old Honest, who has been a traveller
many a day, recalls the many kinds of pilgrims
he has seen. "I have seen some that have set out
as if they would drive all the world afore them,
who yet have, in few days, died as they in the
wilderness, and so never got sight of the promised land. I have seen some that have promised
nothing, at the first setting out to be pilgrims,
and that one would have thought could not have
lived a day, that have yet proved very good pilgrims. I have seen some that have run hastily
forward, that again have, after a little time, run
as fast just back again. I have seen some who
have spoken very well of a pilgrim's life at first,
that, after a while, have spoken as much against
it. I have heard some, when they first set out
for Paradise, say positively there is such a place,
who, when they have been almost there, have
come back again and said there is none. I have
heard some vaunt what they would do in case
they should be opposed, that have even at a
false alarm fled faith, the pilgrim's way, and
all."

Faithful, through the experience of persecution and martyrdom, reaches the Celestial City
before Christian. Faithful had had no trouble
at the Slough of Despond, nor had he been

accosted by Worldly Wiseman; he had missed the illumination and guidance that Christian was given by the Interpreter and by the maidens of the Palace Beautiful. He had, however, resisted the wiles of Madam Wanton and Adam the First, and proved himself superior to the taunts of Shame. Christian had not met these. Sunshine was with Faithful through the dark valleys which Christian had found so terrifying. Yet behind the multitude that witnessed his cruel death the Dreamer saw "a chariot and a couple of horses waiting for Faithful, who was taken up into it and straightway was carried up through the clouds with sound of trumpet *the nearest way to the Celestial gate."*

Then there is Hopeful, too, whose cheer and counsel Christian needs. His optimistic nature led him into faults, and without Christian, as he acknowledges, he would have been in danger of death. In Doubting Castle Christian contemplates suicide and it needs Hopeful's arguments to "moderate his mind." While we deplore the fate of Ignorance, whom we saw carried off to hell just as he thought heaven would open its gates to him, we welcome Hopeful's optimism when he tells Christian, as they leave Vanity Fair together, he is sure many of the foolish people of the town will "take their time and follow after." At the river they must both cross "a great darkness and horror" fell upon Christian "so that he could not see before him." He forgot the "sweet refreshments that he had met with in the way of his pilgrimage," and "Hopeful had here much ado to keep his brother's head above water." Hopeful it was who cried, "Be of good cheer, my brother; I feel the bottom, and it is good." So Christian's experience need not be universal. It is, indeed, not the highest. Mr. Valiant-for-truth crosses with greater confidence and greater honour, and when Mr. Stand-fast goes over there is "a great calm at that time in the river."

We have seen how, unlike the Puritan of stage caricatures, Bunyan (with the wisdom of his later years, when he produced the Second Part of *Pilgrim's Progress*) found a place in the pilgrimage for joy and music; and, too, how tenderly his Great-heart and the Lord of all pilgrims deal with weaklings like Fearing, Feeble-mind, Ready-to-halt, and Despondency. We may add that he saw, as few of his co-religionists could see, that (despite the implications of St. Paul's injunctions) women are truly "sharers with us in the grace of life." It was with an unusual delicacy that he portrayed his women characters; even Madam Wanton is described with restraint and Christiana is made to think kindly of the poor woman.

The appeal of Bunyan's works to the humble folk of the cottages and servants' halls of England is not surprising. His masterpiece, which before he died had reached a circulation in cheap editions of a hundred thousand copies—and that in the seventeenth century—is an epic of the domestic life and deals with man as man, apart from social distinctions. It discovers greatness in common people of the lowliest station. It holds up an ideal of the Christian life which does not restrict its joys and rewards to men privileged by education or high birth. Although in his prologue to the Second Part Bunyan says,

Young ladies and young gentlewomen too,
Do no small kindness to my Pilgrim show;
Their cabinets, their bosoms, and their hearts
My Pilgrim has, . . .

it remains true that the story was not mentioned in polite society, nor discovered by literary critics, till the late eighteenth century. "Perhaps," says Macaulay, it is "the only book about which, after the lapse of a hundred years, the educated minority has come over to the opinion of the common people."

We come, finally, to Bunyan's thought about the Church and its ministry. Chaucer in his picture of the poor parson and Herbert in his *Temple* had given literary expression to ideals for the clergy, and others were to follow. Bunyan, however, was the most fertile in imagery and the most searching in critical insight. His minister (in the composite picture reached by combining Evangelist, Help, the portrait seen in the House of the Interpreter, the four Shepherds, Knowledge, Experience, Watchful, and Sincere, and, last but not least, Great-heart, the preacher-soldier) suggests the minister of Hawthorne's *Mosses from an Old Manse,* "not estranged from human life, yet enveloped in the midst of it with a veil woven of intermingled gloom and brightness." Bunyan owed much, though perhaps less than he supposed, to "the holy Mr. Gifford's" counsel, and repays his obligation by showing his pilgrims much indebted to their ministerial guides.

The church Bunyan pictures in the Palace Beautiful. There Christian is well entertained by Prudence, Piety, and Charity, and finds a fellowship so congenial that he is willing to rest a while. His bed-chamber is called Peace and there is a broad vista of Immanuel's Land from the top of the house. In clear weather the Delectable Mountains can be seen. Within the house are ancient records and the relics of prophets, apostles, and martyrs. In Beulah the pilgrims could not yet "with open face" behold the City save "through an instrument made for that purpose." In the Second Part monuments are frequently seen; Bunyan's sense of the continuity of the spiritual life across the ages apparently developed through his pastoral experience. He saw even more clearly the value of guidance and tradition. When Christiana and Mercy leave the Palace Beautiful a "scheme" is put into their hands; it is the church that can provide them with a map. Perhaps the shepherd boy clad "in very mean clothes, but of a very fresh and well-favoured countenance," who has "more of that herb called Heart's ease" in his bosom than many that are finely clad, may represent the country parsons. Bunyan himself refused more than one call to London. When Christiana receives her summons to cross the river, she asks Great-heart how she may best prepare for her journey.

With this clearly-indicated respect for the church, however, Bunyan saw the dangers in ecclesiastical form and organization, which were in his days so great. It was, indeed, his protest against the surrender of the church to worldly and political intrigues that cost him twelve years of imprisonment. He had at one time greatly reverenced the outward show and state of the church, but the little company of Bedford dissenters led him to take a quite other view. Formalist, he tells us, was "lost in a great wood" when he essayed what he thought was a short cut to avoid the hill Difficulty, and Hypocrisy, taking still another way, "stumbled and fell and rose no more." Bunyan saw formalism not only in the Established Church of his day but on the Puritan side too. In a work of 1685, on the much discussed question of the Sabbath, he says that he is reluctant to enter on a question of such trifling moment—the question which day, Saturday or Sunday, is the true Sabbath—and that he is sorry to see fictions and factions growing amongst Christian men "to the loss of that good spirit of love and that oneness that formerly was with good men." He had objected vigorously enough to the formal, set prayers of the Book

of Common Prayer, appointing as it did "such
a prayer for such a day and that twenty years
before it comes"; but he saw that there was another extreme. In *The Pharisee and the Pub-
lican* (1685) he said,

It is at this day wonderful common for men
to pray extempore also. To pray by a book, by
a premeditated set form, is now out of fashion.
He is counted nobody now, that cannot at any
moment, at a minute's warning, make a prayer
of half an hour long. I am not against extempore prayer, for I believe it to be the best kind
of praying; but yet I am jealous that there are
a great many such prayers made, especially in
pulpits and public meetings, without the breath-
ing of the Holy Ghost in them. For if a Pharisee
of old could do so, why may not a Pharisee do
the same now? . . . Great is the formality of
religion this day and little the power thereof.

Bunyan was fortunate in his association
with a church which at its very inception chose
a broad and inclusive covenant as the basis of
its fellowship. "The principle," say the church
records, upon which the founders "entered into
fellowship one with another, upon which they
did afterwards receive those that were added to

their body and fellowship, was faith in Christ and holiness of life, *without respect to this or that circumstance or opinion in outward and circumstiall things.*" By this means "disputings and occasions to janglings and unprofitable questions" were avoided. John Gifford, on his death-bed, wrote a letter to the congregation which is still read once every year. "When you are met as a church there's neither rich nor poor, bond nor free, in Christ Jesus. 'Tis not good practice to be offering places or seats when those who are rich come in; especially it is a great evil to take notice of such in time of prayer, or the word. . . . Then are bowings and civil observances at such times not of God." Division about unessential matters Gifford declared to be a great evil.

In this democracy of free opinion and mutual respect Bunyan's spiritual life was nourished. When some tried to draw him into a discussion of questions of baptism, he wrote (in *A Confession of Faith,* 1672) that if they wished to know by what name he would be distinguished from others he would tell them plainly. "I tell you I would be, and hope I am, a Christian, and choose, if God should count me worthy, to be called a Christian, a believer, or other such name which is approved by the Holy Ghost. And as for these titles of Anabaptist, Independent, Presbyterian or the like, I conclude that they came neither from Jerusalem nor Antioch, but rather from hell and Babylon, for they naturally tend to divisions. You may know them by their fruits."

He employed a pretty fancy to suggest that Christians should be like flowers growing in a garden together "that have upon each of them the dew of heaven" and, letting the dew fall upon each other's roots, "are jointly nourished and become nourishers of each other." If this broad charity and inclusiveness had been learned wherever men learned, from the Bible and *Pilgrim's Progress,* the rudiments of their Christian faith, how different might Christian history have been!

Bunyan preached liberty, but he did more than preach. Whittier says, "What Milton and Penn and Locke wrote in definition of Liberty, Bunyan lived out and acted." Bunyan had passed through the stirring experience of conversion from a careless to a devout life. He could speak pointedly and searchingly of the meaning of those events in the soul which happen independently of special and authorized religious observances and which need no priest for their validation. When he was forbidden to testify to others of his joy in serving God he braved a long imprisonment rather than consent to a compromise; he suffered, indeed, beyond most men because he was so staunch and unyielding and, doubtless, because he was known to be effective as an exhorter. He was, in the language of the mittimus under which he was committed to prison, not only one who "devilishly and perniciously abstained from coming to church to hear divine service," but "a common upholder of several unlawful meetings and conventicles, to the great disturbance and distraction of the good subjects of this kingdom." Having refused to make compromises which would have saved him from prison, he could speak with the authority of a man who had proved his sincerity. He became for his own generation, and he remains in days that still see liberty at times in jeopardy, a type of prophetic courage, speaking with the conviction that is born of experience and obedient at any cost to an inward call. His allegory combined with its religious appeal a searching call to men who were in danger of weak com-

pliance when loyalty meant persecution. Would
that the liberty he won and used with charity
might become the possession of all who find a
gospel in his allegory and a challenge in his
example!

BIBLIOGRAPHY

No attempt is made to give an exhaustive bibliography. Most good libraries contain a selection from the many editions of *Pilgrim's Progress; Grace Abounding* and *The Holy War* are less commonly accessible. The New York Library possesses the most complete collection of editions of *Pilgrim's Progress,* including the very rare first edition which is also in the British Museum. Important additions (Worldly Wiseman and By-ends) were made to the third edition, and this also contained a frontispiece portrait of Bunyan asleep as the Dreamer. Few illustrations were added until the eleventh edition, which contained fifteen, one of which is reproduced on page 126. Illustrations from a Dutch edition were borrowed in many English editions of the eighteenth century. See Brown's *John Bunyan,* chap. xix.

I. BUNYAN'S WORKS

The Works of John Bunyan. Editions of Offor (Glasgow, 1856, 3 vols.) and Stebbing (Toronto, 1859, 5 vols., illustrated).

The Pilgrim's Progress and *Grace Abounding* (in one volume, Tercentenary edition, 1928, illustrated). American Tract Soc.

The Pilgrim's Progress (127 illustrations). American Tract Soc.

Other editions of *Pilgrim's Progress* are those published by the Clarendon Press, Oxford (edited by Canon Venables), 1879; Brentano & Company, 1901; The Century Company, 1912 (copiously illustrated); Henry Holt & Company, 1911; T. C. and E. C. Jack, London, 1917. That of H. Virtue & Company, 1901, edited by A. J. Foster, contains interesting references to Bedfordshire and the scenes among which Bunyan grew up.

Inexpensive editions, of convenient size for the pocket, are found in the Golden Treasury Series, Macmillan; Everyman's Library, E. P. Dutton; The Modern Students Library; Charles Scribner's Sons; and the Riverside School Library, Houghton Mifflin Company.

Among editions for children, that published by the Atlantic Monthly Press, edited and abridged by Edith F. Smith, with charming illustrations by Harriet S. Smith, may be specially mentioned.

John Bunyan, A Book for Boys and Girls, American Tract Soc., 1928, edited by E. S. Buchanan, with several colored illustrations, reproduces the original text of a book of verse published by Bunyan two years before his death. Posthumous editions were given the name *Divine Emblems,* and out of Puritan prejudice omitted many of the most characteristic "poems." This volume is of interest in a study of Bunyan's development, revealing a sense of humor unusual in Puritans, but it is not likely to appeal to modern boys and girls in spite of the editor's enthusiastic introduction.

The Holy War and *The Heavenly Footman* (with introduction and notes by Mabel Peacock, Oxford, at the Clarendon Press, 1892).

The Holy War. John C. Winston Co.

II. BIOGRAPHICAL AND CRITICAL ESSAYS

John Bunyan, His Life, Times, and Work. John Brown, D.D., 1886. (The definitive *Life;* lengthy, detailed, interestingly written.)

John Bunyan. J. A. Froude. (English Men of Letters Series.)

John Bunyan and His Church at Bedford. J. Carter. (Pub. in Bedford, 1864; a copy is in the New York Library.)

John Bunyan. By the author of Mark Rutherford.

The Road of Life. (2 vols.) John Kelman.
(Extremely suggestive commentary on *Pilgrim's Progress,* marked by a wealth of literary allusion.)

Bunyan Characters. (2 vols.) Alexander Whyte.
(Very sympathetic study of the men and women Bunyan's Pilgrim meets; strongly evangelical.)

Lectures on the Pilgrim's Progress. G. B. Cheever, 1884.

Poets and Puritans. T. R. Glover.

Saints and Heroes. Vol. 2. George Hodges.

Biographical Essays. G. B. Macaulay.

Familiar Men and Books. R. L. Stevenson.

Classics of the Soul's Quest. R. E. Welsh.

Old Portraits and Modern Sketches. J. G. Whittier.

Eleven Christians. Studies in Personality. Student Christian Movement (London).

Famous Leaders Among Men. S. K. Bolton.

Thirteen Worthies. Llewellyn Powys. (Amer. Library Service, 1923.)

Social Ideals in English Letters. Vida Scudder. (Pages 87 ff.)

Beside Still Waters. A. C. Benson.

III. The History of the Period

For the period of Bunyan's life, with reference to social, political, and religious conditions, the following works will be found useful:

England under the Stuarts. G. M. Trevelyan.
History of England. G. M. Trevelyan, 1927.
History of England. G. B. Macaulay. Ch. ii.
Historical Sketches. Thomas Carlyle.
Of Reformation in England. John Milton.
Life of Col. Hutchinson by his Widow.
Journal. George Fox.
Puritan and Anglican. E. Dowden.
English Democratic Ideas in the Seventeenth Century. G. P. Gooch.

The following relics of Bunyan are preserved in the Manse of the Bunyan Meeting at Bedford: The Record Book of the Church, with a number of entries in Bunyan's handwriting; his will; a cabinet, a staff, and a jug which belonged to him; and many editions and translations of *Pilgrim's Progress.* In the vestry of the Bunyan Meeting are Bunyan's chair (see page 54) and a massive door originally in the gaol in which *Pilgrim's Progress* was written. At the Institute in Bedford is the three-volume Fox's *Book of Martyrs* which Bunyan took with him to prison and on the pages of which he wrote comments in prose and verse. At the Record Office in London is Bunyan's application on behalf of himself and others for licenses to preach (see page 91).